ROUTLEDGE LIBRARY EDITIONS:
PSYCHOLOGY OF EDUCATION

Volume 41

THE PSYCHOLOGY OF EDUCATIONAL TECHNOLOGY AND INSTRUCTIONAL MEDIA

THE PSYCHOLOGY OF EDUCATIONAL TECHNOLOGY AND INSTRUCTIONAL MEDIA

KEN SPENCER

Routledge
Taylor & Francis Group
LONDON AND NEW YORK

First published in 1988 by Routledge

This edition first published in 2018
by Routledge
2 Park Square, Milton Park, Abingdon, Oxon OX14 4RN

and by Routledge
711 Third Avenue, New York, NY 10017

Routledge is an imprint of the Taylor & Francis Group, an informa business

British Library Cataloguing in Publication Data
A catalogue record for this book is available from the British Library

ISBN: 978-1-138-24157-2 (Set)
ISBN: 978-1-315-10703-5 (Set) (ebk)
ISBN: 978-1-138-70975-1 (Volume 41) (hbk)
ISBN: 978-1-315-20083-5 (Volume 41) (ebk)

THE PSYCHOLOGY OF EDUCATIONAL TECHNOLOGY AND INSTRUCTIONAL MEDIA

KEN SPENCER

ROUTLEDGE
London and New York

First published in 1988 by
Routledge
11 New Fetter Lane, London EC4P 4EE

Published in the USA by
Routledge
in association with Routledge, Chapman & Hall, Inc.
29 West 35th Street, New York NY 10001

British Library Cataloguing in Publication Data

Spencer, Ken
The psychology of educational technology and instructional media.
1. Educational technology — Psychological aspects
I. Title
371.3'07'8 LB1028.3

ISBN 0-415-00567-1

Library of Congress Cataloging-in-Publication Data

ISBN 0-415-00567-1

Printed and bound in Great Britain by
Biddles Ltd, Guildford and King's Lynn

CONTENTS

ACKNOWLEDGEMENTS

My thanks are due to the many colleagues and friends who have contributed, some unknowingly, to this book: especially Carol, Anna and Jane. Over the years I have received encouragement from Ann Clarke and inspiration from Janet Duffin, whose insights have promoted the educational rather than the instructional aspect of Educational Technology. The original idea for the book stemmed from a meeting sponsored by the Council for Educational Technology, and I am grateful to all members of CET who have worked so hard at promoting this field. I could not have developed the initial idea without the feedback from my students, and I thank all who have suffered during the past few years. Without the computer wizardry of Phil Wade I could not have met my deadlines: thanks, Phil! And, finally, special thanks to Derek Packham, who read the draft and provided many valuable comments and suggestions; however, the final responsibility for both content and treatment must remain entirely my own.

CHAPTER 1

THE EVOLUTION OF EDUCATIONAL TECHNOLOGY

Educational technology is composed of at least two overlapping subsets: technology in education and technology of education. The tools-technology, sometimes known as the hardware approach to educational technology, but more commonly known under the title audio-visual aids or instructional media, may be thought of as technology in education. Whereas, the educational application of knowledge from the behavioural sciences, such as psychology, forms the basis of a technology of education.

Educational technology can be seen as an umbrella term for the application of scientific knowledge in the field of education. This covers considerable ground, as can be seen in Figure 1-1, which lists some of the areas for inclusion in Hilgard's (1964) instructional technology and in Figure 1-2, which identifies crucial disciplines which impinge on Hawkridge's (1981) concept of educational technology.

Jonassen (1985) has discussed the psycho-philosophical perspective of educational technology in this century, showing the various shifts in theoretical foundations and practices associated with four distinct phases: the physical science or instructional media movement, the behaviourist and neo-behaviourist movements, and finally the constructivist or cognitive science approach.

The physical science approach gained momentum early in the century as the audiovisual movement, focusing on the machines and materials, rather than the learner (Saettler, 1968). This approach was concerned with the effects of devices and procedures, which were seen as acting as an antidote to the excessive verbalism of traditional teaching methods (Wittich and Schuller, 1953). The new media were to supply a concrete basis for conceptual thinking, make learning more permanent, develop continuity of thought, the growth of meaning and efficiency, depth, and variety of learning (Dale, 1954). It yielded to the behaviourist approach following the training effort of World War 2, culminating in the 'systems approach' to course design in the 1960's. In many ways this remains the corner-stone of educational technology. It was grounded historically in behaviourism and later developed by behavioural psychologists who explicitly excluded the study of mental processes, placing emphasis only on observable changes in behaviour. This aspect of educational technology is most obvious in the linear teaching machines devised by B.F. Skinner.

There has been a gradual reaction to this radical

Figure 1-1. Components of Educational Technology: Physical and behavioural sciences. (Based on Hilgard, 1964)

Physical sciences and technologies

Optics:	projected pictures (still and moving)
Chemistry:	paper, ink, photography
Electronics:	sound recording, television, complex teaching machines
Mechanical Engineering:	printing press, movable type, movies, sound recording
Electrical Engineering:	sound films, sound recording, television

Mathematics

Probability & statistics:	experimental design

Behavioural sciences

Psychology:	Individual differences, psychometrics, learning theory, task analysis, instructional media research, teaching machines

---

behaviourism resulting in what has been termed neo-behaviourism, which acknowledges that behaviour is all we can observe, but claims that the observed behaviour depends on mental processes. It is at this stage of evolution that educational technology is to be found in its present form, according to Jonassen.

However, there has been a major revolution going on in psychology for several decades, which has replaced the mechanistic behaviourist model of human behaviour with the constructivist model. Here the individual is seen to select and interpret the raw materials of experience, which are ultimately transformed into different realities for different people. Piaget (1970) says that knowing reality is a process of constructing systems of transformations that model reality. This cognitive model of learning has largely replaced behaviourism and is now in the process of being assimilated into the technology of education. If this occurs to any great extent the goal of replication of behavioural responses will be replaced by the activation of covert

Figure 1-2. Components of Educational Technology: Elements of a concept map. (Based on Hawkridge, 1981)

Methods of learning:

cognitive psychology, learning styles, interaction analysis, gaming/simulation, communication theory, linguistics, textual communications, artificial intelligence, information processing

Objectives for learners:

systems theory, epistemology, politics, philosophy, sociology

Evaluation of teaching and learning:

cost-benefit/effectiveness analysis, economics, attitude and opinion research, social psychology, teacher evaluation, content analysis, measurement of learning, psychological measurement, psychology, mathematics and statistics, computing

Environments:

group dynamics, logistics, individualised learning, anthropology

Media for learning:

design, graphics, electronics, engineering, production techniques

---

mental processes required to build an appropriate cognitive model of reality within the learner.

Hilgard's early formulation is mainly composed of those physical sciences which contribute to the production of educational hardware or machines, and those behavioural aspects which are associated with the first three stages in the evolution of educational technology: from the physical science approach to the neo-behaviourist approach.

Hawkridge's later drawing of the educational technology map is much more comprehensive, covering most of Hilgard's earlier formulation and extending it to include anthropology, sociology, philosophy and politics. Psychology is particularly well-represented, including cognitive psychology in addition to those aspects traditionally associated with educational technology.

In the following chapters the evolution of educational technology in its various guises will be considered from the psychologist's point of view, but first it is necessary to introduce the three major psychological theorists whose early work profoundly affected the development of educational technology throughout most of this century.

Thorndike, Edward Lee (1874-1949)

Although later known for his pedagogical teachings, Thorndike was initially concerned, not with human learning and its educational implications, but with animal learning and intelligence. His learning theory, one which was to dominate all others in America for a quarter of a century, was first announced in his doctoral dissertation 'Animal Intelligence' (1898). This was profoundly affected by Darwinian theory, which, according to Thorndike, provided psychology with the evolutionary point of view.

> .... the mind's present can be fully understood only in the light of its total past.
>
> Psychology has by no means fully mastered this lesson. Human learning is still too often described with total neglect of animal learning. But each decade since The Origin Of The Species appeared has shown a well marked increase in comparative and genetic psychology. (Thorndike, 1909, p.65-80)

He began his work in order to provide a mechanistic account of animal learning, which could be stated in terms of elementary operations and events, and was concerned to dispel the myth of animal ratiocinative intelligence. This led to his detailed study of what was later called trial-and-error learning.

In a typical experiment a hungry cat or dog was placed in a box similar to that shown in Figure 1-3. The door was pulled open by a weight attached to a string as soon as the animal loosened the bolt or bar which held it shut. A dozen or so variations of the box were used, some having loops of wire, in various positions in the cage, attached by string to latches, others having wooden buttons or catches close to the door, and others with levers or platforms inside the box operating release mechanisms. A final version had the experimenter release the door when the animals engaged in a specific activity, such as licking or scratching themselves.

Initially the animals engaged in much unsuccessful and irrelevant behaviour before the door latch was tripped in an almost accidental manner, and Thorndike provides a vivid account of that behaviour:

Figure 1-3. Thorndike's puzzle box. (Based on Thorndike, 1898)

When put into the box the cat would show signs of discomfort and of an impulse to escape from confinement. It tries to squeeze through any opening; it claws and bites at the bars or wire; it thrusts its paws out through any opening and claws at everything it reaches; it continues its efforts when it strikes anything loose and shaky; it may claw at things in the box. It does not pay very much attention to the food outside, but seems simply to strive instinctively to escape from confinement. The vigour with which it struggles is extraordinary. For eight or ten minutes it will claw and bite and squeeze incessantly.... The cat that is clawing all over the box in her impulsive struggle will probably claw the string or loop or button so as to open the door. And gradually all the other non-successful impulses will be stamped out and the particular impulse leading to the successful act will be stamped in by the resulting pleasure, until, after many trials, the cat will, when put in the box, immediately claw the button or loop in a definite way.

The starting point for the formation of any association in these cases, then, is the set of instinctive activities which are aroused when a cat

> feels discomfort in the box either because of confinement or a desire for food. (Thorndike, 1898, p.13)

The times taken for the animal to escape were high at first but on succeeding trials times for escape decreased, remaining relatively stable after 10-20 trials. The associative processes, which Thorndike was concerned to study, showed a gradual stamping in of correct responses and stamping out of incorrect responses, according to the commensurate pleasure (or lack of it) resulting from the response. It was from these studies with animals that the first scientific theory of learning emerged, Thorndike's theory of connectionism:

> I have spoken all along of the connection between the situation and a certain impulse and act being stamped in when pleasure results from the act and stamped out when it doesn't. (Thorndike, 1898, p.103)

This 'law of effect', as it was to be called, brought motivation and reward to the foreground of experimental psychology. Rewards, or successes and failures, provided a mechanism for the selection of the more adaptive responses, and this bears much resemblance to the mechanism of 'natural selection by successful adaptation', which was the basis for Darwin's theory of evolution. This law augmented the familiar law of habit formation through repetition, for Thorndike, and the two became central to his theories of learning and instruction, when he joined the faculty of Teachers College, Columbia University, in 1899, where he shifted his emphasis from animal to human learning.

> The Law of Effect: The Law of Effect is that, other things being equal, the greater the satisfyingness of the state of affairs which accompanies or follows a given response to a certain situation, the more likely that response is to be made to that situation in the future.
> The Law of Exercise: All changes that are produced in human intellect, character and skill happen in accord with and as a result of, certain fundamental laws of change. The first is the Law of Exercise, that, other things being equal, the oftener or more emphatically a given response is connected with a certain situation, the more likely it is to be made to that situation in the future.... This law may be more briefly stated as: 'Other things being equal, exercise strengthens the bond between situation and response.' (Thorndike, 1912, pp.95-96)

The kinds of phenomena coming under the law of exercise are those repetitive habits such as rote memorization or the acquisition of muscular skills. The belief being simply that, as the old saying has it, 'Practice makes perfect.' From this it is predicted that learning curves plotting performance against practice trials should increase in accord with the law. Forgetting curves will show the opposite tendency with a loss of skill over various intervals.

A third law, the law of readiness, was an accessory principle which characterizes the conditions under which there is satisfaction or annoyance. It was couched in rather dubious neuro-physiological terms which can be paraphrased as follows:

1. Given the arousal of an impulse to a particular sequence of actions, the smooth carrying out of the sequence is satisfying.
2. If the sequence is blocked, that is annoying.
3. If the action is fatigued or satiated, then forced repetition is annoying.

Here, Thorndike was suggesting that satisfaction and frustration or annoyance depend on the state of readiness of the organism when a particular response occurs.

These laws of connection forming or association or habit furnished education with two obvious general rules, according to Thorndike: (1) put together what should go together and keep apart what should not go together, (2) reward desirable connections and make undesirable connections produce discomfort. In other words, exercise and reward desirable connections and prevent or punish undesirable connections. He felt that although such rules or principles may seem obvious the fact was that an examination of the literature of educational theory, at that time, would prove that they were neglected and misunderstood, and that practical use of them was never made.

However, these simple laws, derived from his early research in the animal laboratory, were placed in the context of the complexities of human learning, where four varieties of learning could be distinguished: (1) connection-forming of the common animal type, as is found when the ten-month-old baby learns to beat a drum, (2) connection-forming of ideas, as when a two-year-old learns to think of its mother upon hearing the word 'mother', (3) analysis or abstraction, as when a student of music learns to respond to an overtone in a given sound, and (4) selective thinking or reasoning, as when a language student learns the meaning of a sentence by using his knowledge of the rules of syntax.

His advice to the teacher was not limited to the application of his major laws. The active role of the learner, who comes to the learning situation with a constellation of motivational variables was also recognized by Thorndike and he listed five aids to improvement in learning, which he believed were accepted by educators, and which will surely stand scrutiny today (1913, pp.217-226):

1. Interest in the work
2. Interest in improvement in performance
3. Significance of the lesson for some goal of the student
4. Problem attitude in which the student is made aware of a need which will be satisfied by learning the lesson
5. Attentiveness to the work

Unfortunately, his laws of learning did not stand the test of time. To Thorndike's credit, he was prepared to acknowledge his errors and, in 1929, before the International Congress of Psychology in New Haven, he admitted that he was wrong and introduced two fundamental revisions of his laws of exercise and effect.

It became apparent that exercise alone will not necessarily produce improved performance. For example, if a blindfolded subject is asked to attempt to draw a line of a given length, and to do so hundreds of times, over many days, but without information concerning the accuracy of his performance, there is no improvement in the ability to draw the line of correct length during the experiment. Feedback is clearly an essential component . Thorndike (1931) quotes an experiment in which a long series of word-number pairs were presented to the subjects. If repetition alone produced the stamping in of associations then each of the pairs (number-word, word-number) should have been recalled with equal strength. They were not, and it was clear that the subject's mental set and expectations guided the associations formed.

A number of experiments also demonstrated that the effects of reward and punishment are not equal and opposite. Instead, under several conditions, reward was found to be much more powerful than punishment. One such experiment (1932) used a simple maze which gave chicks a choice of three pathways, one of which led to 'freedom, food and company.' The wrong choices led to confinement for thirty seconds. Thorndike concluded that:

> The results of all comparisons by all methods tell the same story. Rewarding a connection always strengthened it substantially; punishing it weakened it little or not at all. (Thorndike, 1932, p.58)

Similar effects were found with human subjects learning

word translations, the rewarded responses (experimenter saying 'Right') led to repetition of the rewarded condition, but the punished condition ('Wrong') did not weaken the connections.

Thorndike went on to collect a series of testimonials about the relative effects of rewards and punishments from published biographies and other sources and found almost universal evidence of the greater beneficial effect of reward than punishment (1935, pp.135-144, 248-255).

These changes in the laws of learning occurred at a time when Thorndike's proposals for the development of a science and technology of instruction were being eclipsed by the rise of the new school of psychology, J. B. Watson's 'Behaviourism.'

His contribution to modern instructional technology, however, cannot be overestimated. He was the undisputed originator of the first scientific theory of learning and, as such, his influence has been profound and long-lasting, not least because of his prescience concerning the potential of technology in the pedagogical process. As early as 1912 he suggested that:

> Great economies are possible by printing aids, and personal comment and question should be saved to do what only it can do. A human being should not be wasted in doing what forty sheets of paper or two phonographs can do. Just because personal teaching is precious and can do what books and apparatus cannot, it should be saved for its peculiar work. The best teacher uses books and appliances as well as his own insight, sympathy, and magnetism. (Thorndike, 1912, p.167)

Saettler (1968) claims that in his three-volumed work, 'Educational Psychology' (1913), Thorndike formulated the basic principles underlying a technology of instruction. In implementing these principles Thorndike suggested that control of the learning may not be the sole responsibility of the teacher and that machines could play a part. He proposed what may be considered the earliest example of programmed learning in his influential text 'Education' (1912):

> If, by a miracle of mechanical ingenuity, a book could be arranged that only to him who had done what was directed on page one would page two become visible, and so on, much that now requires personal instruction could be managed by print. (Thorndike, 1912, p.165)

He was also an advocate of the laboratory method where students examined real things and observed them working rather than merely speculating or arguing about them. He suggested that there are certain elements of knowledge, certain tendencies to respond, which can only be got by direct experience of real things.

> This fact may, and should, now seem axiomatic, but many teachers in practice forget it, and teachers a few centuries ago rarely thought about it. The increased use of methods whereby the realities are examined and experimented with as well as talked about, enormously improved the teaching of mathematics, science, history and even language. (Thorndike, 1912, p.176)

However, he also advised that verbal methods were not always wrong, nor that a pupil should always be provided with the direct experience itself. He anticipated the later audio-visual movement with his claim that different degrees of reality may be desirable - the actual thing or a model of it, a photograph or a rough sketch or even a map of it (1912, p.177). He also cautioned against the unbridled use of the popular discovery methods and suggested that if the doctrine is taken literally 'it becomes absurd', and that:

> It would be enormously costly thus to deprive children of the advantages of civilization, and would be the height of folly, even if it could be done at no cost. (Thorndike, 1912, p.194)

In fact, in his early work, Thorndike sees much to commend those methods embodying 'telling and showing', such as lectures and demonstrations but also including the use of printed text-books, object lessons, maps, dictionaries and tables of logarithms, all of which are 'clear cases of the lecture-demonstration or telling-showing method' (1912, p.189). He acknowledged the criticisms that the student may see or hear but not understand and that he does not learn to think but concluded that 'the chief excellence of this method is economy.... in some cases this advantage alone justifies its use' (1912, p.189).

Pavlov, Ivan Petrovich (1849-1936)

Pavlov, the father of Russian psychology, initially trained and worked as a physiologist. He gradually changed his interest in favour of psychology following the incidental observation of the phenomena we now know as the conditioned reflex. His influence on psychology has been profound and long-lasting. In fact, Kimble (1961) found that 31 terms relevant to conditioning and learning are directly attributable to Pavlov, and only 21 terms to all American and Western psychologists combined. He was awarded the Nobel

Prize in 1904 for 'The Work of the Digestive Glands' (1897), the first Russian scientist, and the first physiologist in the world, to receive the award.

In his student years Pavlov was attracted to the philosophy of materialism, particularly as embodied in the work of Claude Bernard, which suggested that the science of living phenomena must have the same foundations as the science of inorganic bodies and that there is no difference between the principles of biological science and those of physico-chemical science.

A particularly strong influence on Pavlov was the physiologist I.M. Sechenov, who conducted a series of experimental investigations of the nervous system and its reflexes in Bernard's laboratory in 1862. He tried to publish the results of this work in a widely read Moscow review under the title 'An Attempt to Establish the Physiological Basis of Psychical Processes.' However, the tsarist censor realized that Sechenov's intention was to spread materialistic ideas concerning the relationship between physiology and psychic activity, and would only permit publication in a specialist medical journal under the title 'Reflexes of the Brain.' The article represented a daring challenge to the deeply entrenched Cartesian doctrine of psycho-physiological parallelism, that body and mind comprise two completely separate and materially unrelated systems, which somehow run on parallel tracks and, when it eventually appeared in book form, it again produced a reactionary outcry from the Petersburgh Censorial Committee, on the grounds that it destroyed the religious doctrine of eternal life. This was just four years after Darwin's 'Origin of the Species' (1859), which taught that all phenomena have a history including origin and development from lower forms, had shaken the foundation of the creationist religious dogma. Sechenov's book, which supported Darwin's ideas, eventually became a popular classic of the time and Sechenov passed the remaining years of his academic life as Professor of Physiology at Moscow University.

Sechenov proposed that all the immense diversity of psychical phenomena can and must be explained on the basis of the nervous system and the brain, through the mechanism of reflex arcs. He suggested that thought and emotion can be accounted for in terms of the reflex, by analogy with lower forms, but it was Pavlov who provided experimental proof of this with the discovery of the conditioned reflex.

Entering the University of St. Petersburgh to study natural science, Pavlov's early interest in physiology flourished and he received a gold medal for his experimental work on the physiology of the nerves of the pancreas. In 1875 he received his degree, with an outstanding record of achievement. By 1890 Pavlov had perfected a method for studying the nervous regulation of the blood, with animals trained to undergo all the manipulations of a long and complex experiment without narcosis. From 1891 he was head of the Department of Physiology in the new Institute of Experimental Medicine, and it was here that he conducted his work on the digestive glands. Pavlov found that vivisectional methods were unsuitable for studying the intricate workings of the digestive system and so he perfected the 'chronic' experimental method, begun in his work on the circulatory system. This involved the creation, through highly skilled surgery, of a fistula, an opening or a window which allowed the experimenter to observe the functioning of the gland under controlled conditions, but in a normal healthy animal.

By 1901 Pavlov became engrossed in a problem which he had deferred investigating, but which was to lead to the discovery of the conditioned reflex, to which he devoted the remaining 35 years of his life.

During his experimental work Pavlov had found that gastric juice was secreted by experimental dogs not only when food was introduced into the mouth but also when they saw the food. This action at a distance, through the eyes, ears and nose was generally interpreted in terms of the so-called higher functions and was considered to be far beyond the reach of physiology.

Animal psychology was not on an objective experimental basis at this time, Thorndike's 'Animal Intelligence' had only recently been published and was not available to Pavlov. At first, Pavlov suggested that the observed anticipation and consequent salivation must be acquired with the aid of the higher functions - the animals judgement, will and desires, but he soon distanced himself from such a view:

> To understand these phenomena, are we obliged to enter into the inner state of the animal and to fancy his feelings and wishes as based on our own? For the investigator, I believe there is only one possible answer to the last question - an absolute "No."
> .... In our "psychical" experiments on the salivary glands (we shall provisionally use the word "psychical"), at first we honestly endeavoured to explain our results by fancying the subjective condition of the animal. But nothing came of it except unsuccessful controversies, and individual, personal, inco-ordinated opinions. We had no alternative but to place the investigation on a purely objective basis. (Pavlov, 1928, p.50)

The psychical experiments demonstrated that it was not just the appearance of the food, its odour etc. which produced salivation, but 'absolutely all the surroundings in which these objects are presented to the dog, or the circumstances with which they are connected in real life'(p.52). For example, the dish, the room, the person who usually fed the animal and the noises produced by him. Pavlov recognized the adaptive value of such reactions to 'remote signs (signals).' In fact, this adaptive reflex was originally termed condition<u>al</u> and not condition<u>ed</u> by Pavlov, in his address on the occasion of receiving the Nobel Prize. However, 'conditioned' reflex has become fixed in English usage. The conditioning procedure is shown in Figure 1-4.

> A further essential difference between the old and the new reflexes is that the former are constant and unconditional, while the latter are subject to fluctuation, and dependent upon many conditions. They, therefore, deserve the name "conditional" (ooslovny). (Pavlov, 1928, p.79)

Figure 1-4. Pavlov's Conditioning Procedure.

Meat Powder (unconditioned stimulus)	-------->	Salivation (response which is an unconditioned response)
Meat Powder + Sound of bell (neutral stimulus)	-------->	Salivation
Sound of bell (conditioned stimulus)	-------->	Salivation, after repeated pairings (conditioned response)

The great discovery made by Pavlov was that any stimulus, even one not remotely connected with an inborn reflex, when paired with a stimulus inextricably linked to an inborn reflex response, could take the place of the original stimulus. In this case, the sound of the bell (originally neutral, producing no salivation) is repeatedly paired with meat powder (the unconditioned stimulus) which calls forth the salivation reflex. Following repeated pairings, the sound of the bell acquires the power to evoke the salivation reflex, even in the absence of meat powder.

It is, in effect, acting as a signal for the meat powder, producing an anticipatory response.

By 1904, Pavlov was discussing the importance of the signals which stand in place of the unconditioned stimulus in the reflex. These signals can have only a conditional significance and are readily subjected to change, for example, when the sound of the bell is not accompanied by meat powder the salivation response is gradually weakened, a process termed 'extinction.' And this is precisely how adaptive advantage is conferred. In the wild a startle or fear response may be evoked in an animal by any number of stimuli presented by a predator, those which are repeatedly present are strengthened as signals, while others of an incidental nature are extinguished.

Pavlov decided that organisms must possess two sets of reflexes. A fixed set of simple, inherited reflexes and a set of acquired, conditioned reflexes formed by the pairing of previously neutral stimuli with a stimulus which triggers off a simple reflex. The conditioned reflexes were found to be routed through the cerebral hemispheres, causing Pavlov to suggest that:

> The central physiological phenomenon in the normal work of the cerebral hemispheres is that which we have termed the 'conditioned reflex.' This is a temporary nervous connection between numberless agents in the animal's external environment, which are received by the receptors of the given animal, and the definite activities of the organism. This phenomenon is called by psychologists 'association'....The basic physiological function of the cerebral hemispheres throughout the.... individual's life consists in a constant addition of numberless signalling conditioned stimuli to the limited number of the initial inborn unconditioned stimuli, in other words, in constantly supplementing the unconditioned reflexes by conditioned ones. Thus, the objects of the instincts exert an influence on the organism in ever-widening regions of nature by means of more and more diverse signs or signals, both simple and complex; consequently, the instincts are more and more fully and perfectly satisfied, ie., the organism is more reliably preserved in the surrounding nature. (Pavlov, 1955, p.272-273)

The organism is sensitized to signals in the environment which help in the avoidance of pain and difficulties and lead to the things needed for the preservation of the individual and perpetuation of the species. Pavlov felt that all complex learned behaviour is composed of orchestrated simple reflexes, which are physiological, rather than mental, processes. From this it followed that objective investigations would lead, ultimately, to the prediction of all human and animal behaviour. In this, Pavlov paved the way for an objective science of behaviour which was to appeal to Watson and the behaviourists later in the century.

Watson, John B. (1878-1958)

John B. Watson is generally accorded the distinction of being the founder of 'Behaviourism.' His early work was concerned with ethological studies of the behaviour of birds in the wild, and laboratory learning experiments with white rats in mazes, which earned him his doctorate in 1903. His major impact was made with the so-called manifesto for behaviourism: Psychology as the Behaviourist Views It (1913), in which he was not proposing a new science as such, but was arguing that psychology should be redefined as the 'study of behaviour' rather than the science of the 'phenomena of consciousness.'

> Psychology as the behaviourist views it is a purely objective experimental branch of natural science. Its theoretical goal is the prediction and control of behaviour. Introspection forms no essential part of its methods, nor is the scientific value of its data dependent upon the readiness with which they lend themselves to interpretation in terms of consciousness. The behaviourist, in his efforts to get a unitary scheme of animal response, recognizes no dividing line between man and brute. The behaviour of man, with all of its refinements and complexity, forms only a part of the behaviourist's total scheme of investigation. (Watson, 1913, p.158)

Just as Thorndike had sought to rid psychology of speculations concerning animal consciousness and thought, so Watson wished to circumvent human consciousness in favour of an objective study of behaviour alone. He wished psychology to turn away from the introspectionist psychology of Wundt and Titchener. Wundt had set up the world's first formal laboratory of psychology in Leipzig and had started the first effective journal for experimental psychology, but his work and that of his followers, including Titchener at Cornell University's laboratory of experimental psychology, failed to live up to Watson's expectations:

> It was the boast of Wundt's students, in 1879, when the first psychological laboratory was established, that psychology had at last become a science without a soul. For fifty years we have kept this pseudo-science, exactly as Wundt laid it down. All that Wundt and his

> students really accomplished was to substitute for the word "soul" the word "consciousness." (Watson, 1925, p.5)

Watson felt that one can assume either the presence or absence of consciousness anywhere in the phylogenetic scale, without it influencing the study of behaviour or the behaviouristic experimental method. The emphasis on human consciousness as the centre of reference for all behaviour caused him to draw the analogy with the Darwinian movement and its initial concern with material which contributed to an understanding of the origin and development of the human race. However, the moment zoology undertook the experimental study of evolution and descent, the situation immediately changed and data was accumulated from the study of many species of plants and animals, with the laws of inheritance being worked out for the particular type under investigation. Such studies were of equal value when compared with those dealing with human evolution.

The new brand of psychology was also to provide an answer to the question 'What is the bearing of animal work upon human psychology?' which, Watson admitted, had caused him some embarrassment. He suggested that for a fusion of animal and human studies to occur some kind of compromise was necessary: either psychology would have to change its viewpoint so as to take into account facts of behaviour, whether or not they had bearings upon the problems of consciousness; or else behaviour would have to stand alone as a wholly separate and independent science. Watson declared that should there be a failure of 'human psychologists' to accommodate, the behaviourists would be driven to using methods of investigation comparable to those employed in animal work, with human subjects.

Watson's quarrel was not with the systematic and structural introspectionists alone. It was also with the new styled functionalist school, which was supposed to throw light on the biological significance of consciousness instead of its analysis into structural elements. Watson found, having done his best to understand the difference between structural and functional psychology, that 'instead of clarity, confusion grows in me.'

He was concerned, ultimately, to unite such diverse studies as the paramecium response to light, learning problems in rats and plateaus in human learning curves, but in each case by direct observation and under experimental conditions. This psychology would be undertaken in terms of stimulus and response, habit formation, habit integrations and the like. It would take as a starting point, first, the observable fact that organisms, man and animal alike, adjust to their environments by two means: hereditary and habit. Secondly, that certain stimuli lead organisms to make responses. Such a system of psychology, Watson believed, when completely worked out would enable the stimulus to be predicted, given the response; or, given the stimulus, the response could be predicted. Watson makes clear what it is he really requires of psychology:

> In the main, my desire in all such work is to gain an accurate knowledge of adjustments and the stimuli calling them forth. My final reason for this is to learn general and particular methods by which I may control behaviour. (Watson, 1913, p.168)

If psychology were to take such a path there would be practical benefits, which Watson put into effect in 1920, when he was forced to leave the academic life following a scandalous affair with a former pupil: he became an advertising man. He felt that, with such a psychology, the educator, the physician, the jurist and the businessman could utilize the data in a practical way. In pedagogy, for example, the psychologist may endeavour to find out 'by experimentation whether a series of stanzas may be acquired more readily if the whole is learned at once, or whether it is more advantageous to learn each stanza separately and then pass to the succeeding one' (p.169). The psychologist would not attempt to apply the findings, they would merely be made available to the teacher, application of the principle being purely voluntary.

But who would fail to apply the principles and powerful techniques which Watson had in mind for his new psychology? Conditioning was to play a significant role in this psychology as Watson made clear two years after his 'somewhat impolite papers against current methods in psychology' (1916, p.89). He felt it incumbent upon himself to suggest some method which might be used in place of introspection, following his criticisms. Conditioned reflexes were claimed to be suitable for providing the possibility of objectively approaching many problems in psychology. Using such methods Watson claimed that he gave no more instruction to the human subjects than he gave to the animal subjects; nor did he care what language the subject spoke or whether he spoke at all. The conditioned reflexes enabled Watson to 'tap certain reservoirs which have hitherto been tapped only by the introspective method.'

It was, however, Watson's conditioning of Little Albert which has attracted most attention, and has been enshrined in the history of psychology (Watson and Watson, 1921). Albert was eleven months old when he first entered Watson's laboratory. A small, white rat was shown to the boy, whose natural tendency was to stretch out his hands to touch and play with the animal. Watson documented this response, identifying it as that of a normal child, who is curious and reacts positively to the rat. A few days later the boy and the rat were brought together in the same room, but with a rather bizarre difference. Each time the child reached for the rat Watson banged a long steel bar very loudly with a carpenter's hammer, causing the infant to jump violently and fall forward 'burying his face in the mattress.' After a short interval the boy again reached out to the animal - and Watson repeated his routine with the hammer. 'Again the infant jumped violently, fell forward and began to whimper.' Little Albert was so disturbed that no further tests took place for a week.

At first, when boy and rat were reunited, Albert did not reach out for the rat. Eventually, when the rat was placed near to him, he began to reach out towards it, very gingerly, then he began playing with blocks in a normal way. Watson now showed Albert the rat three times and accompanied each presentation with the same loud noise. The child puckered his face, whimpered and withdrew his body. This procedure was repeated on a further three occasions, until as soon as the child saw the rat he began to cry and crawl away so rapidly that he was 'caught with difficulty before he reached the edge of the mattress.'

Watson claimed that this demonstrated an explanatory principle of how our emotions originate. The conditioned response generalized to other animals, including a rabbit and a dog, and even a fur coat, and survived intact for more than a week. Watson did intend de-conditioning the child, but Little Albert was adopted by a family living some distance from the laboratory, and may, even at the time of writing, survive with his fear intact!

Building on his success with Little Albert and other similar conditioning and de-conditioning experiments, and following on from the claims made by Pavlov, which suggested the powerful influences of the environment on an organism's behaviour through the agency of conditioning, Watson proposed a daring challenge, epitomizing the empiricist tradition:

> Give me a dozen healthy infants, well-formed, and my own specified world to bring them up in and I'll guarantee to take any one at random and train him to become any type of specialist I might select - doctor, lawyer, artist, merchant-chief and, yes, even beggar-man and thief, regardless of his talents, penchants, tendencies, abilities, vocations, and race of his ancestors. (1925, p.82)

The work of Thorndike, Pavlov and Watson made psychology a respectable science in which phylogenetic continuity was an essential ingredient, permitting extrapolation from the results of animal experimentation to the complex domains of human behaviour. And nowhere was this more apparent than in the emergence of B.F. Skinner's radical behaviourism, and its educational manifestation: the linear teaching machine.

REFERENCES

Cohen, D. (1979) J.B. Watson: The Founder Of Behaviourism. London: Routledge and Kegan Paul.

Dale, E. (1954) Audiovisual Methods In Teaching. London: Holt, Rinehart and Winston.

Hawkridge, D.G. (1981) 'The telesis of educational technology', British Journal of Educational Technology, 12(1), 4-18.

Hilgard, E.R. (1964) Theories Of Learning and Instruction. Chicago: University of Chicago Press.

Jonassen, D.H. (1985) 'Learning strategies: a new educational technology', Programmed Learning And Educational Technology, 22(1), 26-34.

Kimble, G.A. (1961) Hilgard And Marquis' Conditioning And Learning. New York: Appleton-Century-Crofts.

Pavlov, I.P. (1897/1902) The Work Of The Digestive Glands. London: Griffin.

Pavlov, I.P. (1928) Lectures On Conditioned Reflexes. (Translated by W.H. Gantt) London: Allen and Unwin.

Pavlov, I.P. (1955) Selected Works. Moscow: Foreign Languages Publishing House.

Piaget, J. (1970) Genetic Epistemology. New York: Columbia University.

Saettler, P. (1968) A History Of Instructional Technology. New York: McGraw-Hill.

Thorndike, E.L. (1898) 'Animal Intelligence', Psychological Review, Monograph Supplement, 2, No. 8.

Thorndike, E.L. (1909/1962) 'Darwin's contribution to psychology', University of California Chronicle, 12, 65-80. In G.E. Joncich (Ed) Psychology And The Science Of Education. New York: Columbia University.

Thorndike, E.L. (1912) Education: A First Book. New York: Macmillan.

Thorndike, E.L. (1913) Educational Psychology. New York: Teachers College, Columbia University.

Thorndike, E.L. (1931/1966) Human Learning. Cambridge: MIT Press.

Thorndike, E.L. (1932) 'Reward and punishment in animal learning', Comparative Psychological Monographs, 8(9).

Thorndike, E.L. (1935) The Psychology Of Wants, Interests And Attitudes. New York: Appleton-Century-Crofts.

Watson, J.B. (1913) 'Psychology as the behaviourist views it', Psychological Review, 20, 158-178.

Watson, J.B. (1916) 'The place of the conditioned reflex in psychology', Psychological Review, 23(2), 89-117.

Watson, J.B. (1925) Behaviourism. London: Kegan Paul, Trench and Trubner.
Watson, J.B. and Watson, R. (1921) 'Studies in infant psychology', Scientific Monthly, Dec., 493-515.
Wittich, W.A. and Schuller, C.F. (1953) Audio-visual Materials: Their Nature And Use. N.Y.: Harper.

CHAPTER 2

THE ART OF TEACHING AND THE SCIENCE OF LEARNING

B.F. Skinner took up the ideas of behaviourism in the 1930's and after extensive experimental research, much of it based on the performance of laboratory rats and pigeons, extended his conclusions to the higher reaches of the phylogenetic chain, to human behaviour.

Skinner's success is attributable to his isolation of a few highly repeatable phenomena in conditioning - many of which Pavlov and Thorndike had studied and named before him (Hilgard and Bower, 1975) - which were then used as a basis for analyzing more complex forms of behaviour. Following on from Watson's psychology, Skinner continued to reject mentalistic or cognitive explanations of behaviour and was interested only in the observable and repeatable.

Operant Conditioning

His early work made extensive use of a piece of apparatus which is now commonly termed the 'Skinner box', shown in Figure 2-1. In such a box, the caged animal (usually a rat or pigeon) presses a lever or pecks at a key and receives food pellets as a reward. It is from this experimental base that Skinner developed the linear teaching machine. A close look at the procedures involved in this 'operant conditioning' is required to appreciate the evolution of such machines, and subsequent criticisms of their use.

The type of conditioning studied by Skinner is similar to the trial and error learning discussed by Thorndike (1898). This differs from Pavlov's procedure in that the confined animal emits the response (presses the lever) which is, according to Skinner, under 'voluntary' control. Whereas classical or Pavlovian conditioning is 'involuntary' and the response is under the control of the autonomic system; it consists of elicited behaviour, such as salivary secretion or pupillary constriction to light.

At the start of the operant conditioning procedure for a rat an unconditioned, hungry animal is placed in the Skinner box. Initially, the rat is encouraged to associate the sound of the food magazine with the delivery of food pellets in the food tray. Pellets are discharged from the magazine periodically by the experimenter to encourage this. During the preliminary training the lever is disconnected from the magazine and at this stage the delivery of food is not contingent upon any behaviour exhibited by the rat.

Figure 2-1. The Skinner Box.

When the rat has been adapted to the environment and moves to the food tray each time it hears the magazine in operation, operant conditioning can begin. The lever is connected to the food magazine so that each time the lever is depressed by the rat a pellet of food is dispensed at the food tray. The rat can then be left to explore the environment. It will show a rather low rate of lever pressing as it explores, but not a zero rate. It will press the lever a few times during an hour at a rather irregular rate (Skinner, 1938) and in doing so will receive the pellet of food, which will act as a reinforcer of the behaviour which immediately preceded it (the pressing of the lever), making it more likely to be repeated. Eventually, the relationship between lever pressing and dispensing of food is made and the rat presses the lever at an increasing rate, as described by Skinner:

> On the first day of conditioning a first response was made five minutes after release. The reinforcement had no observable effect upon the behaviour. A second response was made 51.5 minutes later, also without effect. A third was made 47.5 minutes later followed by a fourth 25 minutes after that. The fourth response was followed by an appreciable increase in rate showing a swift acceleration to a maximum. The intervals elapsing

> before the fifth, sixth, and following responses were 43, 21, 28, 10, 10 and 15 seconds respectively. (Skinner, 1938, p.67-68)

Shaping Behaviour

Not all behaviours can be considered to be discrete units and for some behaviours the experimenter may have to wait hours, days or even weeks before they emerge. The original probability of the response in its final form is very low; in some cases it may even be zero. Fortunately, there is a procedure for producing the response more quickly, the experimenter takes control of the food magazine by disconnecting the lever from the food magazine and rewards successive approximations to the desired response.

> To get the pigeon to peck the spot as quickly as possible we proceed as follows: We first give the bird food when it turns slightly in the direction of the spot from any part of the cage. This increases the frequency of such behaviour. We then withhold reinforcement until a slight movement is made towards the spot.... We continue by reinforcing positions successively closer to the spot, then by reinforcing only when the head is moved slightly forward, and finally only when the beak actually makes contact with the spot. We may reach this final response in a remarkably short time. (Skinner, 1953, p.92)

This procedure is termed 'shaping' the behaviour and it enables the experimenter to bring a rare response to a very high probability in a short time. Having established the response the pigeon will continue pecking the key and receiving food until sated. The animal is usually reduced to 80% of its normal body weight in order to provide the motivation necessary to maintain the lever pressing or key pecking.

Extinction of a Response

If the lever is disconnected from the food magazine the animal's response rate will decline, a property noted by Pavlov, which he termed 'extinction' of the response. This may be used to produce a differential response, as is the case in discrimination training. For example, a pigeon can be trained to peck at a key only when it is illuminated by light of a particular colour (green), but not when it is another colour (red). Initially , it is trained to peck at the unilluminated key until a stable rate is observed. The training then proceeds with a food pellet being delivered for each peck only when it is green. When it is red the animal receives no reinforcement. This soon produces a differential rate of pecking: a high rate for green and an increasingly lower rate to red as the response extinguishes. The special stimulus which must be present in order for a reinforcement to occur (green key) is called a Discriminated Stimulus or S^D.

Schedules of Reinforcement

When each response receives a reinforcement the procedure is termed 'continuous reinforcement'. Of course, under such a schedule of reinforcement the animal soon becomes sated and refrains from responding at a high rate until it is again hungry. Skinner discovered that a high rate of responding could be maintained under a variety of reinforcement schedules, without the necessity to reward each and every response, a technique that 'gets more responses out of an organism in return for a given number of reinforcements' (Skinner, 1953, p.99).

He distinguished between schedules which are controlled by the system outside the organism and those controlled by the animal's behaviour. An example of the first is a schedule based on the passage of time, eg. the animal receives a reinforcement every 5 minutes. When a reinforcement is given every fiftieth response, it is an example of the second type of control. Both types of these 'intermittent schedules' can be either fixed or variable. Thus, a reinforcement in a fixed interval schedule is given after the set time has elapsed, eg. every five minutes; with a variable-interval schedule the reinforcement is given **on average** after a set time, eg. on average every five minutes, with the intervening interval varying between a few seconds or as long as ten minutes. This type of schedule produces behaviour which is extraordinarily persistent and very difficult to extinguish. A fixed ratio schedule also produces a very high rate of response, but the most powerful of all the schedules is the variable-ratio, where the reinforcement occurs after a given number of responses **on average**, the pigeon or rat becoming a victim of an unpredictable contingency of reinforcement.

Cultural Engineering

The results of Skinner's early work were published in his 'Behavior of Organisms' (1938), but his next major work is a somewhat startling contrast, until it is realized that Skinner's first career was journalism. 'Walden Two' (1948), a novel, was written as a programme that outlined the utopia attainable by adopting a behaviouristic, experimental approach toward social problems. The scientists in 'Walden Two' dispensed with traditional 'trial-and-error' freedom because there were efficient ways of attaining desired goals, based mainly on positive reinforcement. Cultural engineering was not a pejorative term in this brave new society, although the book was frequently read as a dystopia. A more technical treatment of the 'Walden Two' ideas is to be found in 'Science and Human Behaviour' (1953), dedicated to his colleague Fred Keller, who later developed the Personalized System of Instruction (see Chapter 4), based on Skinnerian principles. In the section dealing with education, he refers to 'knowledge' as 'the entity which is traditionally said to be maximized by education' (p.408). He acknowledges that it is a complex term, but continues with the assertion that most knowledge acquired in education is verbal. He claims that the acquisition of such knowledge does not mean that education is merely rote learning, because the student also comes to understand the facts. For example, in the study of history this is because:

> The individual agrees with a statement about a historical event in the sense that he shows high probability of making the statement himself. The growing understanding with which he reads and re-reads a passage describing a period in history may also be identified with the growing probability that he will emit verbal responses similar to those which comprise the passage. (Skinner, 1953, p.409)

The Appliance of Science to Teaching

With such a view, linking verbal behaviour to knowledge as the entity to be maximized in education, the stage is set for one of the most important announcements in the history of educational technology. 'The Science of Learning and the Art of Teaching' (1954) was first read at a conference at the University of Pittsburgh, in March, during which there was a demonstration of an experimental teaching machine. It was published later in the year in the influential 'Harvard Educational Review.'

Skinner claimed that it was a great shock to turn from the exciting prospect of an advancing science of learning to that branch of technology which is most directly concerned with the learning process, education. In the first place he questioned the reinforcements used, though he did acknowledge that they had changed since the early years of the century and were not all based on major aversive methods of control, now they were based on 'minor' aversive events such as the teacher's displeasure, low marks etc. He then asked how the contingencies of reinforcement were arranged, for example, when is an arithmetical operation reinforced as 'right'? The conclusion was that many minutes and in many cases many hours or even days may intervene between a child's response and the teacher's reinforcement, even though it could be demonstrated that, unless explicit mediating behaviour has been set up, the lapse of only a few seconds between response and reinforcement destroys most of the effect. He calculated that during the first four years of education 50,000 reinforcements would be necessary to attain efficient mathematical behaviour, but that in a traditional class situation it would be possible for the teacher to provide a pupil with only a few thousand. In order to provide sufficient reinforcements the only possible conclusion was that human learning would require instrumental aid, and the simple fact was that 'as a mere reinforcing mechanism, the teacher is out of date' (Skinner, 1954, p.94).

With the introduction of instrumental aid complex patterns of behaviour could receive gradual elaboration, with the whole process of becoming competent in any field being divided into a very large number of very small steps. The maintenance of the behaviour in strength at each stage could be accomplished by applying the techniques of scheduling which had been developed in the studies of other animals, but more probably would be most effectively arranged through the design of the material to be learned.

> By making each successive step as small as possible, the frequency of reinforcement can be raised to a maximum, while the aversive consequences of being wrong are reduced to a minimum. (Skinner, 1954, p.94)

Skinner demonstrated two prototype machines at Pittsburgh. The first taught arithmetic, with the material to be learned appearing in a square window. Missing numbers were made to appear by moving sliders with numbers printed on. When the problem was completed the child turned a knob on the front of the machine. The machine 'senses the composed answer, and if it is correct, the knob turns freely and a new frame of material moves into place.' It would not turn if the answer was incorrect and the child could then re-set the sliders until a correct answer was obtained. Errors were recorded automatically. The second machine was similar, but with more sliders and was designed to teach both arithmetic and spelling.

Skinner foresaw objections to the use of such devices in the classroom, including the challenge that children were being treated as mere animals and that an essentially human intellectual achievement was being analysed in unduly mechanistic terms. He countered this by suggesting that the behaviours elicited by the instrumental aids were the 'very behaviours which are taken to be the evidences of such mental states or processes' and that the 'behaviour in terms of which human thinking must eventually be defined is worth treating in its own right as a substantial goal of education' (1954, p.96).

With regard to possible costs, he argued that a country which annually produces millions of fridges, automatic dishwashers and washing machines can certainly afford the equipment necessary to promote high standards of education.

Echoing Thorndike he stated that the teacher has a more important function than to say 'right' or 'wrong' and that 'it is beneath the dignity of any intelligent person' to mark a set of papers in arithmetic. The more important work, the teacher's relations with her pupils, cannot be duplicated by a machine, and instrumental help would improve these relations by freeing the teacher. He concluded:

> There is a simple job to be done. The task can be stated in concrete terms. The necessary techniques are known. Nothing stands in the way but cultural inertia. But what is more characteristic of the modern temper than an unwillingness to accept the traditional as inevitable? We are on the threshold of an exciting and revolutionary period, in which the scientific study of man will be put to work in man's best interests. Education must play its part. (Skinner, 1954, p.97.)

With the new technology, which was to apply the newly emerging science of learning to the age-old art of teaching, we can see how Skinner drew parallels between his work with animals and the action of an ideal teaching environment. As with the animals in the Skinner box the human learner must make a response which is observable and can be described in operational terms. The learner's behaviour is shaped by the programme, which consists of discriminated stimuli (programme frames), with the correct responses being immediately reinforced (knowledge of results), on a continuous schedule. Incorrect responses are extinguished, because they receive no reinforcement.

Within a few years there was such interest in programmed learning that Schramm (1964) in his review of the research concluded that 'no method of instruction has ever come into use surrounded by so much research activity.' By 1957 Skinner was demonstrating a machine in which a frame of material appeared in a window near the centre of the machine and the student wrote his answer in a window to one side of the frame. By moving a lever the response made by the student moved under a transparent cover (it could be seen, but not altered, making the device cheat-proof) and at the same time the correct response was uncovered in the upper corner of the frame. If the student recognized that his response was correct he moved another lever which punched a hole next to the correct response and shifted the programme on to the next frame. Such machines were used to teach a course in human behaviour to Skinner's Harvard University students, with nearly 200 students completing the course.

Skinner compared the machine to a private tutor because there is constant interchange between programme and student, unlike lectures and textbooks. The programme 'insists' that a given point be thoroughly understood and presents just sufficient material for which the student is ready, thus ensuring that the student comes up with the correct answer, which receives positive reinforcement and holds the student's interest, according to Skinner.

It was eventually realized that the essential feature of the new method of teaching was the 'programme' rather than the machine and this led to the development of the programmed linear text in which 'frames' were printed on one side of the page and answers on the reverse, a form used in Holland and Skinner's influential text 'The Analysis of Behavior: a program for self-instruction' (1961).

The Research: Does It Work?

The major research question in the decade that followed Skinner's announcement of the forthcoming revolution in education was 'Do students learn from programmed instruction?' Claims were made that student performance could be increased, giving 90% of students scores of 90% on evaluation tests, and the commercial stakes were high, particularly for companies with educational interests. Schramm (1964) attempted to answer this question and located 190 reports of original research on programmed instruction, which included some experiments with programmed films and television. Most of the research (40%) was conducted with college students as subjects, with smaller numbers of secondary (20%) and adult/military (20%) subjects and a minority of primary/pre-school (10%) subjects. From this mixture of research Schramm concluded that many different kinds of students - college, high school, secondary, primary, pre-school, adult, professional, skilled labour, clerical employees, military, deaf, retarded, imprisoned - do indeed learn from linear programmes either on machines or as texts. Using programmes such students learned mathematics and science at different levels, foreign languages, spelling, electronics, computer science, psychology, statistics, business skills, reading, and many other subjects. For each of the groups of students and the different kinds of subject matter the early experimental evidence demonstrated that 'a considerable amount of learning can be derived from programmes' (Schramm, 1964, p.4) either by comparing pre- and post-tests or the time and trials to reach a given criterion of performance.

When the question is changed to 'How well do students learn from programmes as compared to how well they learn from other kinds of instruction?' Schramm could not answer quite so confidently. Of the 36 studies which compared programmed instruction with traditional teaching, 18 showed no significant statistical difference when the two groups were measured on the same criterion test. But 17 showed a statistically significant superiority in favour of the programmes, with only one showing a difference in favour of classroom students. Schramm cautiously concluded that 'the results should not discourage us about the amount of learning derived from programmes' (p. 5).

In addition to the question of comparative effectiveness researchers were also investigating the nature of the components of the teaching programme. There are six components of an efficient linear programme (1) an ordered sequence of items, through which the student works, (2) at his own pace, in (3) short steps (4) making few errors in his (5) written, constructed responses, to which he receives (6) immediate knowledge of results. Each has received attention in experimental evaluations of the effectiveness of programmed instruction.

A Logical Sequence?

Five interesting experiments compared logically sequenced programmes with a presentation of the items in random order and, surprisingly, three of the experiments showed no difference, one showed no difference on a retention test and the remaining comparison showed a difference in favour of the logical structure. The results were obtained with short programmes and it was concluded that longer programmes would require a more ordered sequence. Gagné and his collaborators (Gagné, 1962a; Gagné and Paradise, 1961; Gagné et al, 1962) analyzed a number of tasks (solving algebraic equations) and found evidence for hierarchies of subordinate learning sets, thus providing a basis for logical structure within programmes. A subordinate learning set being defined as what the subject needed to know in order to be able to perform a new task. However, Mager (1961a) complicated matters by demonstrating that when students in an electronics course were given a free hand to learn by questioning an instructor, they took a path which bore little resemblance to the logical sequence in which the course was taught. The instructors tended to move from parts to wholes, whereas the students typically moved from smaller wholes to larger wholes. A seemingly straightforward issue was not resolved by these competing results. Mager captured their essence when he claimed that:

> Where it is necessary to teach one thing before another, do so. But be careful! There isn't as much reason for this kind of sequencing as instructors like to think. (Mager, 1961b)

Later, McKeachie (1974a) also commented on the ability of learners to withstand quite considerable distortions of the original programme sequences, suggesting that the motivational effect of 'surprisingness' is sometimes neglected and that 'randomness may not make sense conceptually but it may be more fun than a sequence so logical and with steps so small that one knows exactly what is coming next.'

A Self-paced System?

It was assumed that a major advantage of the new technology would be that the student could proceed at her own pace. Surprisingly, the early research failed to confirm this. Seven of the studies found no difference between external and individual pacing, with students taught by machine, text or television, compared with two studies in favour of individualised pacing. Carpenter and Greenhill (1963) varied the pace from 20 percent below to 10 percent above the average of class self-pacing without decreasing the overall amount of learning. Hartley (1974), in a later review of the research from 1954-1974, also found a wealth of non-significant differences in test performance between individual and group learning in either paced or unpaced situations, and concluded that the research indicated three main points:

> (i) Self-pacing produces considerable administrative difficulties, because even like-ability groups spread out enormously in terms of time taken to complete a programme.
> (ii) Group-pacing methods are often technically complex to set up: the gains (if any) may not be worth the technical effort involved.
> (iii) Some learners have difficulty in judging what is an appropriate pace at which to go.
> (Hartley, 1974, p.281)

The last point has implications for programme writers because, although the learner can control the speed at which he works through the programme, the overall pace is largely determined by the writer.

Short Steps?

Skinner proposed that programmes should have short steps, which would lead to few errors in the learning sequence and, initially, this was controlled by the physical size of the frame window in a Skinner machine. Much of the early evidence supported short step size. Evans, Glaser and Homme (1960) tested programmes teaching conversion to unfamiliar number bases, with 30, 40, 51 and 68 steps and found the 51 and 68 step versions to be superior to the others on both immediate and delayed retention. Coulson and Silberman (1960) obtained similar results for programmes teaching psychology items. But, Smith and Moore (1961) found no difference when teaching spelling by means of programmes of 1, 128, 830 and 546 steps.

One of the most fascinating series of early experiments employed training films, such as the assembly of an automobile ignition distributor (Maccoby and Sheffield, 1958; Margolius and Sheffield, 1961; and Weiss, Maccoby and Sheffield, 1961). The length of film viewed before permitting practice was varied in each experiment and it was found that more learning came from gradually increasing step size rather than from maintaining short or long steps. When the students were given control of the film sequence, they also gradually increased the length. Students only permitted to practice short steps showed a gradually deteriorating performance, adding to a body of evidence suggesting student impatience and boredom with long programmes having only short steps.

Although the balance of the early studies was in favour of short steps, Hartley suggested that the following issues were also important:

- (i) the ability of the learners involved (university students found small steps irritating)
- (ii) the age of the learners (small steps were more appropriate for small children)
- (iii) the pre-knowledge of the learners (small steps were more suitable than large steps for learners with little relevant background)
- (iv) the confidence of the learners (small steps were more suitable for learners who were afraid of the task in hand - eg. statistics for female arts undergraduates)
- (v) the kind of subject matter (small steps might be useful for statistics, or for subjects with their own built-in logic, but not for more over-

inclusive subjects such as, for example, literary appreciation)

(vi) the language employed (complex language can still be confusing even in small steps).
(Hartley, 1974, p. 282)

An Active Response?

One of the major differences between operant and classical Pavlovian conditioning was claimed by Skinner to be the active, 'voluntary' response of the animal to a given stimulus. This aspect of the early animal research is included in programmed instruction by the demand for an overt, observable, constructed response, usually a written response to a stimulus item in the programme. Unfortunately, this characteristic of the linear programme was by no means unequivocally supported by the early research. The great majority of the studies showed no statistically significant differences between the amount learned from overt and covert responses. Schramm identified 16 research investigations demonstrating this result. Since there was no difference, and since covert or 'thinking' the response took less time, the covert mode could be considered more efficient. A minority of cases demonstrated some difference in favour of the overt, constructed response, mainly for complex subject matter (Cummings and Goldstein, 1962).

Pressey (1963) offered a direct challenge to the Skinnerian programme ideal when he tested the first unit of the Holland-Skinner psychology programme (54 frames) against the same material re-written in good prose paragraphs. There was no difference in the final performance, but the prose version took less time for the students. Schramm concluded that the results 'are going to cause researchers in this field to do a great deal of thinking about the principles behind programmed instruction' (p. 10). Of course, when the step size is such that error levels are reduced to a minimum, overt responding may become superfluous.

Leith (1968) demonstrated that the need for overt responding depended on the type of task and the background of the learner. Conceptual tasks, for example, are clearly different from response-learning tasks. English spelling was found to be better accomplished by writing the responses, while co-ordinate geometry or the structure of genetic materials were learned more successfully when covert responses were required. Even recall, retention and transfer of complex circuit diagrams were carried out just as efficiently by thinking the responses as by drawing them if the students had a background of 'O' level Physics. Those students with less than 'O' level knowledge of Physics did poorly when thinking the responses but did as well if allowed to make overt responses.

Hartley (1974) concurred, adding that overt responses may be superior when the learners were young children, when the material was difficult and the programmes lengthy and when novel or specific terminology was taught.

Immediate Knowledge of Results?

The majority of the early studies did support another of the central tenets of Skinnerian programming, the provision of immediate knowledge of results (Schramm, 1964, p.10). Meyer (1961) found significantly more learning from immediate knowledge when compared with a group that waited for the next meeting to receive results. However, not all the research demonstrated advantages for immediate knowledge of results. Glaser and Taber (1961) did not find any difference when the knowledge of results was varied from 100 percent continuous knowledge of results to 50 or 25 percent knowledge, or when it was received in a variable ratio. They concluded that if the probability of error is low, as in typical linear programmes, knowledge of results is less important than when the probability of error is high.

Later studies confirmed the complexity of the issue. Grundin (1969) found that overt responding interacted with frequency of feedback, making the knowledge of results superfluous, or even detrimental. When learners were required to work out each stage of a correction for themselves, receiving feedback stage by stage, Tait, Hartley and Anderson (1973) found that they performed better than learners receiving more global feedback. McKeachie (1974b) commented that

> Programmed instruction proponents were understandably aghast to find that immediate knowledge of the correct response (expected to be a reinforcer) did not facilitate learning in programmed instruction. (p.8)

Intrinsic Programming

One major change in programming styles, which contested the mode of responding, size of step and type of feedback, was introduced by Crowder in the late 1950's. This intrinsic or branching style of programming presents larger amounts of information, usually a paragraph, for the student to study. There is an immediate test, usually a multiple-choice question, and the test result is used to determine the content of the next frame in the teaching sequence. If the answer is correct, she is automatically given the next unit of information and the next question. But if the answer is incorrect the preceding unit of information is reviewed, the nature of the error is explained and she is retested (Crowder, 1960). There is a separate set of correctional materials for each wrong answer that is included in the multiple-choice test.

This 'intrinsic' programming technique was devised to operate with a sophisticated device for handling programmed materials on microfilm, but could equally be applied to what became known as 'scrambled' texts, in which each answer has a different page number associated with it. The student turns to the page number associated with his answer, which may contain the next unit of information, if the answer is correct, or the correctional information followed by the original question, if the answer is wrong.

Crowder claimed that human learning takes place in a variety of ways and that these ways vary with the abilities and knowledge of the students, the nature of the subject matter etc. The intrinsic programming method would provide the necessary feedback control in this complex series of interactions. This is different to simply providing knowledge of results to the student because the test result is used to control the behaviour of the teaching machine, the primary purpose being to determine whether the communication was successful, in order that corrective steps may be taken if it has failed (Crowder, 1960, p.288).

The term 'intrinsic' programming was used to indicate that the necessary programme of alternatives was built into the material itself such that no external programming device was required, in contrast to the early experiments which were using computers as 'extrinsic' programming devices.

Schramm found few research evaluations of the intrinsic methods, but those which were available showed no differences between the two methods. Hartley (1974) agreed with Schramm's overall conclusion concerning the lack of differences between linear and branching programmes, but observed that some studies demonstrated a saving in time taken to complete the programme, in favour of branching programmes, with older and intelligent learners. This strikes at the heart of Skinnerian psychology, because Skinner had argued most strongly for maximizing the positive consequences of learning and a minimizing of the negative aspects.

Few Errors?

The larger frames of information and the method of responding in Crowder's method naturally allows for more errors in the programme, but in this case this is seen to be a positive virtue. Leith (1968) demonstrated that for 10 and

16-year-olds there was no relationship between success on test performance and numbers of errors made. This was confirmed by Elley (1966). A further study by Leith showed that making and overcoming errors may sometimes help learning. Children were taught to calculate in bases other than ten. One group learned four different bases, another learned two (with twice as much practice on each) and a third group learned only one base, but with four times the practice. Each group read the same number of frames. The group with two bases made most errors when they changed to the second base, but were best on a transfer test to an entirely new base.

Having determined that research had indicated that each of the original characteristics was not a sine qua non of programmed learning, Hartley concluded that 'Skinner's techniques have not been shown to be universally valid. They have not, however, been shown to be valueless' (1974, p.286).

The Art of Scientific Application

The results of these early research studies do seem to cast doubt on most of the characteristics of linear programmes, which were derived from Skinner's psychological theories. This may well be because the translation of psychological principles into educational practice has not always been as precise or accurate as Skinner claimed (Bugelski, 1971). For example, linear programmes embody the Skinnerian principle of shaping behaviour, the student being led step by step to the final goal. But in normal laboratory usage shaping refers to a sequential act. The pigeon is trained to turn clockwise in a circle and then to peck at a key and then climb on a perch. When training is completed the acts are carried out in succession by the animal, but this is not so for the student who ends the programme by carrying out a completely new act, one which he may never have carried out before. The student does not go through the entire sequence of steps in the programme when performing the last operations.

Thorndike had used the words 'right' and 'wrong' as rewards and punishments, with the consequence that knowledge of results was adopted as a perfectly satisfactory secondary reinforcer in teaching machines. To Bugelski (1971) the use of knowledge of results as a reinforcer makes it impossible for anyone to determine whether the teaching machine really represents an application of a psychological principle. Indeed, it must be remembered that the animals in Skinner's experiments were reduced to 80% of their normal weight; they were in a deprived state before engaging in the required behaviour and once satisfied stopped performing.

There is also evidence that different groups of students react in different ways to the type of reinforcement or feedback. McKeachie (1974b) reports a number of studies showing that informing a child of the correctness of his response increases achievement for middle class children, while other children may learn more effectively when given praise or tangible rewards. Means and Means (1971) found that below average students did well on a mid-term exam when told that they had previously performed well on an aptitude test; whereas above average students did better when told that they had done poorly on the aptitude test.

Later Research: Meta-analysis

Three decades and more further on there is little discussion concerning the merits of one form or another of programmed instruction. Research peaked in 1967 and has been declining steadily since that date, although there continues to be interest in individualised modes of learning and the old techniques of programming have been given a new lease of life in some applications of computer-based learning.

There are, however, new techniques for evaluating the results of the many early and varied studies of programmed instruction, which attempt to provide estimates of the magnitude of the benefits to be gained from such educational innovations and interventions. Kulik, Cohen and Ebeling (1980) have used a statistical procedure called 'meta-analysis' (Glass, 1976) for the statistical analysis of a large collection of results from individual studies for the purpose of integrating findings. In a traditional review an innovatory method may be shown to be better than a more conventional approach in most cases, but such a review does not say whether the new method wins 'by a nose or a walkaway' (Glass, 1976). Kulik, Cohen and Ebeling calculated the size of the effect of the programmed instruction intervention, using as the index Glass's Effect Size (ES), defined as the difference between the treatment (programmed instruction) and control (traditional classroom) mean scores, divided by the standard deviation of the control group. An effect size of 1.0 would indicate that the difference achieved by the new method is equal to an increase of one standard deviation of the control group's score, shifting the position of an average pupil in the control group from the 50th percentile point to the top 20% of the class. An effect size of 0.8 and above demonstrates a large effect of the experimental treatment, which certainly has educational significance; an ES of 0.2 and less is small and educationally insignificant; an ES of 0.5 is a medium effect and the experimental treatment warrants further investigation and consideration.

Kulik, Cohen and Ebeling (1980) found 56 studies comparing programmed instruction with conventional methods in higher education. A majority of these favoured programmed instruction (40), the remaining 16 favouring conventional methods. Only 25 studies reported statistically significant differences between methods, with 21 favouring programmed instruction. At first sight this seems to produce a very favourable result for programmed instruction. However, when Glass's Effect Size is calculated it is only 0.24. In other words, the effect of programmed instruction in a typical class is to raise student achievement by about a quarter of a standard deviation unit. This is a small effect in educational terms, according to Cohen (1977), but it does mean that in a programmed class 60% of pupils attain at least the average score of the conventional class, compared with 50% of conventional pupils. Medium to large effects were observed in a third of the studies.

When examination scores were analyzed the average score of the conventional class was 64.8%; the average of the programmed class was 67.1%. The two groups differed by 2.3% points on average, based on scores taken from 56 studies.

The same technique was applied by Kulik, Schwalb and Kulik (1982), but with results from secondary school rather than higher education. A total of 47 studies were analysed, with 23 of the studies favouring programmed instruction and 24 favouring conventional classes. However, only 19 studies reported statistically different results, with a majority (12) favouring programmed instruction. The average value of the Effect Size was 0.08, the typical programmed instruction student gaining an advantage of less than one tenth of a standard deviation unit. Such an effect is trivial. It implies that 53% of programmed students perform at least at the average level of the conventional group, which has 50% of students at this level. The ES did vary from strongly negative to strongly positive and when study features were analyzed size of effect was found to be significantly related to the subject matter taught, with social sciences showing a particularly high effect size of 0.57. For mathematics it was surprisingly small and negative (-0.01) and it was small for the science studies. The conclusion was that:

> in general programmed instruction did not improve the effectiveness of secondary school teaching. In the typical study, programmed instruction failed to raise student achievement on final examinations. It did not make students feel more positively about the subject matter they were studying or about the quality of teaching at their schools. Nor did it reduce the role that aptitude plays in determining how much students

> learn in secondary school classes. (Kulik, Schwalb and Kulik, 1982, p.137)

Finally, the results of studies investigating computer-based learning also contribute to the overall picture of small or trivial effects. Kulik, Bangert and Williams (1983) examined the use of computers in several educational modes: managing, tutoring, simulation, programming and 'drill and practice'. The results for 'drill and practice' are relevant given Skinner's early claim for automation of this aspect of teaching. However, they do not show a great advantage for the computer in this role, with a small average ES of 0.27, when computer and conventional classes were compared.

The results of thirty years of experimental evaluations demonstrate that the expectations set by Skinner for his technological revolution have not been fulfilled. Programmed instruction was supposed to make learning more efficient and enjoyable. The research, however, shows that student reactions to programmed instruction were not discernibly different from reactions of students taught conventionally and that differences in attainment were trivial or small, in educational terms, in most cases. Clearly the job of improving education was more difficult than Skinner had predicted from his animal learning theory.

It may well be that learning theories are irrelevant to the solution of such problems, as Gagné (1962b) and McKeachie (1974b) have suggested. After all, the history of automated instruction goes back at least as far as 1860, before Thorndike's work was published, when Halcyon Skinner developed and patented a device for teaching spelling; and Pressey began building machines, which performed all the essential tasks carried out by later programmed devices, as early as 1915, without a supporting learning theory. Perhaps Leith (1968) is correct in suggesting that 'we have been bamboozled in our interpretation of programmed learning by the colourful exploits of a few flamboyant cheer-leaders.'(p.1)

REFERENCES

Bugelski, B.R. (1971) *The Psychology of Learning Applied to Teaching*. Indianapolis: Bobbs-Merrill.

Carpenter, C.R. and Greenhill, L.P. (1963) *Comparative Research on Methods and Media for Presenting Programmed Courses in Mathematics and English*. University Park, Pa.: Division of Instructional Services, Pennsylvania State University.

Cohen, J. (1977) *Statistical Power Analysis for the Behavioural Sciences*. (Revised edition) New York: Academic Press.

Coulson, J.E. and Silberman, H.F. (1960) 'Effects of three variables in a teaching machine', Journal of Educational Psychology, 51, 135-143.

Crowder, N.A. (1960) 'Automatic tutoring by intrinsic programming'. In A.A. Lumsdaine and R. Glaser (Eds) Teaching Machines and Programmed Learning. Washington, D.C.: Department of Audio-Visual Instruction, National Education Association.

Cummings, A. and Goldstein, L.S. (1962/1964) 'The Effect of Overt and Covert Responding on Two Kinds of Learning Tasks.' In W. Schramm (Ed) The Research on Programmed Learning: an annotated bibliography. (OE-31034) Washington, D.C.: U.S. Department of Health, Education and Welfare.

Elley, W.B. (1966) 'The role of errors in learning with feedback', British Journal of Psychology, 36, 296-300.

Evans, J.L., Glaser, R., and Homme, L.E. (1960) 'An investigation of variation in the properties of verbal learning sequences of the teaching machine type.' In A.A. Lumsdaine and R. Glaser (Eds) Teaching Machines and Programmed Learning. Washington, D.C.: Department of Audio-Visual Instruction, National Education Association.

Gagné, R.M. (1962a) 'The acquisition of knowledge', Psychological Review, 69(4), 355-365.

Gagné, R.M. (1962b) 'Military training and principles of learning', American Psychologist, 17, 83-91.

Gagné, R.M. and Paradise, N.E. (1961) 'Abilities and learning sets in knowledge acquisition', Psychological Monographs, 75(15), No.518.

Gagné, R.M., Mayor, J.R., Garstens, H.L. and Paradise, N.E. (1962) 'Factors in acquiring knowledge of a mathematical task', Psychological Monographs, 76(7), No.526.

Glaser, R. and Taber, J.I. (1961/64) Investigations of the Characteristics of Programmed Learning Sequences. In W. Schramm (Ed) The Research on Programmed Learning: an annotated bibliography. (OE-31034) Washington, D.C.: U.S. Department of Health, Education and Welfare.

Glass, G.V. (1976) 'Primary, secondary, and meta-analysis of research', Educational Researcher, 5, 3-8.

Grundin, H.U. (1969) 'Response mode and information about correct answers in programmed instruction: a discussion of experimental evidence and educational decisions'. In A.P. Mann and C.K. Brunstrom (Eds) Aspects of Educational Technology, III. London: Pitman.

Hartley, J. (1974) 'Programmed instruction 1954-1974: a review', Programmed Learning and Educational Technology, 6(11), 278-291.

Hilgard, E.R. and Bower, G.H. (1975) Theories of Learning. Englewood-Cliffs, N.J.: Prentice-Hall.

Holland, J.G. and Skinner, B.F. (1961) The Analysis of Behaviour. New York: McGraw-Hill

Kulik, C.C., Schwalb, B.J. and Kulik, J.A. (1982) 'Programmed instruction in secondary education: a meta-analysis of evaluation findings', Journal of Educational Research, 75(3), 133-138.

Kulik, J.A., Bangert, R.L. and Williams, G.W. (1983) 'Effects of computer-based teaching on secondary school students', Journal of Educational Psychology, 75(1), 19-26.

Kulik, J.A., Cohen, P.A. and Ebeling, B.J. (1980) 'Effectiveness of programmed instruction in higher education: a meta-analysis of findings', Educational Evaluation and Policy Analysis, 6(2), 51-64.

Leith, G.O.M. (1968) Second Thoughts on Programmed Learning. Occasional paper No.1. London: National Council For Educational Technology.

Maccoby, N. and Sheffield, F.D. (1958) 'Theory and experimental research on the teaching of complex sequential procedures by alternative demonstration and practice'. In G. Finch and F. Cameron (Eds) Symposium on Air Force Human Engineering, Personnel and Training Research. Washington, D.C.: National Academy of Sciences, National Research Council.

McKeachie, W.J. (1974a) 'Instructional psychology', Annual Review of Psychology, 25, 161-193.

McKeachie, W.J. (1974b) 'The decline and fall of the laws of learning', Educational Researcher, 3, 7-11.

Mager, R.F. (1961a) 'On the sequencing of instructional content', Psychological Reports, 405-413.

Mager, R.F. (1961b) 'On the sequencing of instructional content'. In I.K. Davies and J. Hartley (Eds) Contributions to an Educational Technology. London: Butterworths.

Margolius, G.J. and Sheffield, F.D. (1961) 'Optimum methods of combining practice with filmed demonstration in teaching complex response sequences: serial learning of a mechanical assembly task'. In A.A. Lumsdaine (Ed) Student Response in Programmed Instruction. A Symposium on Experimental Studies of Cue and Response Factors in Group and Individual Learning from Instructional Media. Washington, D.C.: National Academy of Sciences, National Research Council.

Means, R.S. and Means, G.H. (1971) 'Achievement as a function of the presence of prior information concerning aptitude', Journal of Educational Psychology, 62, 185-187.

Meyer, S.R. (1961) 'Report on the initial test of a junior high school vocabulary program'. In A.A. Lumsdaine (Ed) Student Response in Programmed Instruction. A Symposium on Experimental Studies of Cue and Response Factors in Group and Individual Learning from Instructional Media.

Washington, D.C.: National Academy of Sciences, National Research Council.

Pressey, S.L. (1963/64) 'A Puncture of the Huge "Programming" Boom?' In W. Schramm (Ed) The Research on Programmed Learning: an annotated bibliography. (OE-31034) Washington, D.C.: U.S. Department of Health, Education and Welfare.

Schramm, W. (1964) The Research on Programmed Learning: an annotated bibliography. (OE-31034) Washington, D.C.: U.S. Department of Health, Education and Welfare.

Skinner, B.F. (1938) The Behaviour of Organisms. N.Y.: Appleton-Century-Croft.

Skinner, B.F. (1948) Walden Two. N.Y.: Macmillan.

Skinner, B.F. (1953) Science and Human Behaviour. N.Y.: Macmillan.

Skinner, B.F. (1954) 'The science of learning and the art of teaching', Harvard Educational review, 24, 86-97.

Skinner, B.F. (1968) The Technology of Teaching. N.Y.: Appleton-Century-Croft.

Smith, W. and Moore, J.W. (1961/1964) 'Size-of-step and Achievement in Programmed Spelling.' Lewisburg, Pa.: Bucknell University. In W. Schramm (Ed) The Research on Programmed Learning: an annotated bibliography. (OE-31034) Washington, D.C.: U.S. Department of Health, Education and Welfare.

Tait, K., Hartley, J.R. and Anderson, R.C. (1973) 'Feedback procedures in computer assisted arithmetic instruction', British Journal of Educational Psychology, 43, 161-171.

Thorndike, E.L. (1898) 'Animal Intelligence', Psychological Review, Monograph Supplement, 2, No.8.

Weiss, W., Maccoby, N. and Sheffield, F.D. (1961) 'Combining practice with demonstration in teaching complex sequences: serial learning of a geometrical construction task'. In A.A. Lumsdaine (Ed) Student Response in Programmed Instruction. A Symposium on Experimental Studies of Cue and Response Factors in Group and Individual Learning from Instructional Media. Washington, D.C.: National Academy of Sciences, National Research Council.

CHAPTER 3

BEHAVIOURAL OBJECTIVES AND SYSTEMATIC INSTRUCTION

Perhaps Skinner was a flamboyant cheer-leader, as Leith suggested. His work, however, did have profound effects on educational thought in a number of ways related to the general concept of programmed learning. Attention was focussed first on the objectives of instruction in a general sense (Bloom et al., 1956), and then on the specific objectives of the behavioural objectives movement (Mager, 1962). The idea of mastery learning, popular in the 1930's but failing because of lack of a technology to sustain it (Block, 1971, p.4), was also resurrected as a corollary of programmed instruction, and with it evolved an interest in learning hierarchies and the structure of knowledge (Gagné and Paradise, 1961). These, in turn, have been influential in the development of systems of learning and instruction (Keller, 1968; Bloom, 1968) which have achieved the improvements in standards of learning which Skinner had hoped to bring about by his technological revolution. Here the emphasis has turned from technology in education, with its emphasis on hardware, to the technology of education.

BLOOM'S TAXONOMY OF OBJECTIVES

The 'Taxonomy of Educational Objectives: Handbook 1: The Cognitive Domain' (1956) arrived at a time when the demand for improvements in the efficiency of education was being made by Skinner and his colleagues. The idea for such a taxonomy came during a meeting of examiners attending the 1948 American Psychological Association Convention. Bloom and thirty-three colleagues met over a five year period to discuss their taxonomy, which was then organised and written by a select committee of five members. The taxonomy was to provide a 'theoretical framework which could be used to facilitate communication among examiners.'

> It is intended to provide for classification of the goals of our educational system. It is expected to be of general help to all teachers, administrators, professional specialists, and research workers who deal with curricular and evaluation problems. It is especially intended to help them discuss these problems with greater precision. (Bloom et al., 1956, p.1)

It was hoped that such ambiguous terms as 'really understand', 'internalize knowledge' and 'grasp the core or

Figure 3-1. Major Classes of Taxonomies of Educational Objectives. (Based on Bloom et al., 1956; Krathwohl et al., 1964; Harrow, 1972)

Bloom et al.: Cognitive Domain

1.00 KNOWLEDGE
2.00 COMPREHENSION
3.00 APPLICATION
4.00 ANALYSIS
5.00 SYNTHESIS
6.00 EVALUATION

Krathwohl et al.: Affective Domain

1.00 RECEIVING (attending)
2.00 RESPONDING
3.00 VALUING
4.00 ORGANISATION
5.00 CHARACTERIZATION BY A VALUE OR VALUE COMPLEX

Harrow: Psychomotor Domain

1.00 REFLEX MOVEMENTS
2.00 BASIC-FUNDAMENTAL MOVEMENTS
3.00 PERCEPTUAL ABILITIES
4.00 PHYSICAL ABILITIES
5.00 SKILLED MOVEMENTS
6.00 NON-DISCURSIVE COMMUNICATION

essence', would be redefined as a set of standard classifications, making exchange of information about curricular development and evaluation more precise. Equally important, the psychological relationships within the taxonomy were seen as forming a basis for psychological investigations to shed light on changes in the learner's behaviour. This aspect of the taxonomy has been pursued in various forms throughout Bloom's extensive involvement in the study of education.

The educational objectives described in the taxonomy were in a behavioural form and were seen as being consistent with relevant and accepted psychological principles and theories (p.6). They were concerned with the changes produced in individuals as a result of educational experiences. In other words, the taxonomy was a classification of behaviours which represented the intended outcomes of the educational process (p. 12). However, it was not intended to evaluate the actual behaviours acquired by the students. The emphasis was on obtaining evidence on the extent to which desired and intended behaviours were learned by students. Determining the appropriate value to be placed on the different degrees of achievement of the objectives of instruction was considered to be a matter of grading or evaluating the performance and as such it was considered to be outside the scope of the taxonomy.

One major principle of the taxonomy, that it should be consistent with the then current understanding of psychological phenomena, was reflected in the behaviourist overtones that it should be applied only to those educational programmes which could be specified in terms of changes in 'intended student behaviours.' It was assumed that these changes in behaviour were changes from the simple to the complex.

> If we view statements of educational objectives as intended behaviours which the student shall display at the end of some period of education, we can then view the process as one of change. As teachers we intend the learning experiences to change the student's behaviour from a simpler type to another more complex one which in some ways at least will include the first type.
> (Bloom et al., 1956, p.16)

This view led to the taxonomy being organised into six major classes (Figure 3-1), with a hierarchical order, the objectives in one class making use of and being built on the behaviours in the preceding classes (p.18). According to Bloom, research showed that there was 'an unmistakable trend pointing toward a hierarchy of classes of behaviour' which was in accordance with the 'Taxonomy Of Educational Objectives: Cognitive Domain.' Similar arrangements were to be found in the second part of the taxonomy dealing with the affective domain (Krathwohl et al., 1964) and the tradition was maintained in the taxonomies of the psychomotor domain developed separately by Simpson (1966) and Harrow (1972).

The cognitive domain was further divided into subclasses and subcategories, giving a more comprehensive picture of each level of the hierarchy. For example, the class 'Knowledge' was divided into two subclasses, each with several subcategories (Figure 3-2).

Davies (1976) maintains that there is also a fundamental division in the cognitive domain, which has been largely overlooked in subsequent literature. It was divided into two broad areas, with the lower area of knowledge dealing with products, where little more than recall and recognition is required. The higher areas deal essentially with intellectual processes and require more complex intellectual

Figure 3-2. Taxonomic Structure of 'Knowledge'. (Bloom at al., 1956)

1.00	KNOWLEDGE
1.10	Knowledge of specifics
1.11	Knowledge of terminology
1.12	Knowledge of specific facts
1.20	**Knowledge of ways and means of dealing with specifics**
1.21	Knowledge of conventions
1.22	Knowledge of trends, sequences
1.23	Knowledge of classifications and categories
1.24	Knowledge of criteria
1.30	Knowledge of the universals and abstractions in a field
1.31	Knowledge of principles, generalizations
1.32	Knowledge of theories and structures

abilities, such as determining relationships between and within the knowledge associations acquired in the lower levels of the domain.

Validity of Bloom's Taxonomy

Kropp and Stoker (1966) tested the validity of the hierarchical arrangement for the cognitive domain. The theoretically expected relative order for the categories Knowledge, Comprehension, Application and Analysis was obtained, but not for Synthesis and Evaluation, which both fell between Knowledge and Comprehension. Madaus, Woods and Nuttall (1973) suggested that the taxonomy had a Y-shaped structure, with the stem formed from Knowledge, Comprehension and Application and subsequently divided into one branch of Analysis and another branch from Synthesis to Evaluation.

Ormell (1974) has also found contradictions in the taxonomy. He believes that certain demands for the Knowledge category are more complex than the demands for Analysis or Evaluation. He has suggested that the hierarchical organisation based on increasing complexity of operations should be abandoned and the taxonomy should be split into six parallel categories, but maintaining the different levels within each category.

The linear assumption has been heavily criticized by a number of philosophers of education. For example, Pring (1971) argues that even 'knowledge of specifics' has a variety of intellectual abilities and skills implicitly associated with it:

> .... for something to be recognized as a fact requires some comprehension of the concepts employed and thus of the conceptual framework within which the concepts operate. Similarly with regard to the knowledge of terminology, it does not make sense to talk of the knowledge of terms or of symbols in isolation from the **working** knowledge of these terms or symbols, that is, from a comprehension of them and thus an ability to apply them. (Pring, 1971, p.90)

Seddon's (1978) appraisal of the cognitive domain dealt critically with the educational issue of communicability and the psychological issue of the cumulative structure of the hierarchy, but also recognized the success of the taxonomy in terms of the considerable impact it has made on educational thought and practice and concluded that it had achieved one of Bloom's criteria for its success:

> The taxonomy must be accepted and used by workers in the field if it is to be regarded as a useful and effective tool. (Bloom et al., 1956, p.24)

Green (1964) was critical of the assumption that the goal of teaching is to change students' behaviour. He argued that the goal was to transform behaviour into action, in other words the goal is the capability, competence or understanding that makes rational action possible, an idea since exploited by Gagné and Briggs (1974) in 'Principles of Instructional Design.'

The fact that the taxonomy chose to classify objectives on the basis of intended behaviours without regard for the particular content has also received wide criticism, as Sockett (1971) makes clear:

> "remembering" is unintelligible just as a psychological process (even if we lay aside its counterpart, forgetting) for we remember **something**, cases of remembering are cases of being **right** about what was or is the case. We cannot posit remembering in any sense **apart** from content. If remembering is thought of as content-free we have an empty concept which could not be even part of an educational objective. (p.20)

Furst views as rather more serious the omissions stemming from the separation of the cognitive, affective and psychomotor domains. This artificial separation prevents some desired outcomes from being encompassed within the cognitive scheme, and he gives examples of those excluded: receptivity and sensitivity, skill in observing and data gathering, 'perceptual' or 'motor' activities, moral concepts, basic democratic values and rationality. But perhaps the most serious omission, for Furst, is the lack of an 'understanding' category. Ormell (1979) also objects to this and does not accept the argument that it was omitted as a major category because it was imprecise and has proposed both a definition and a research strategy for identifying this cognitive element.

Travers (1980) does not see it as a true taxonomy at all, and claims that although the major categories give the appearance of a continuum of complexity, it is more akin to an 'inventory of educational customs.' He feels that it lacks the theoretical under-pinnings of true taxonomies.

However, despite such criticisms, even Furst (1981) acknowledges that:

> A handbook that has had over a million copies sold, been translated into several languages, used worldwide, and cited thousands of times hardly needs extensive documentation on its usefulness. (p.448)

OBJECTIVES: A HISTORICAL PERSPECTIVE

The idea for educational objectives was not a new one, and Bloom et al. acknowledged their debt to many authors, particularly Ralph Tyler, to whom the first volume was dedicated. Davies (1976) traces the influences back to Cicero's six divisions of a speech, which were used by Herbart (1924) in his five stages of preparation for lessons. Earlier, Herbert Spencer (1910) had called for a curriculum based on the 'things it most concerns us to know', given that we do not have sufficient time to master all subjects.

Franklin Bobbitt (1924), professor of education at the University of Chicago, took the idea of objectives a stage further, insisting that, in an age of science, exactness and particularity were demanded. He even went so far as to report a list of objectives for each of the major occupations in Indianapolis, which would be needed by children when they left school. These included, for example, the ability to sharpen, adjust, clean, lubricate, replace worn or broken parts, and otherwise keep household and garden tools and appliances in good order and good working condition.

Werrett Charters (1924) extended this scientific perspective, using techniques of job analysis, to argue that individual tasks should be broken down to enable the student to learn without assistance. He suggested seven steps in the construction of a curriculum. First, the major objectives were to be determined; then, these were to be analysed to the level of working units; the working units were to be arranged in order of importance, first for adults and then for children; the number of items capable of being learned in school were selected; the best methods for teaching these items were to be determined; and, finally, the items were to be assembled in an order according to the nature of the children.

Tyler's Principles of Objectives

Bobbitt and Charters were recommending a behavioural approach to curriculum design, founded on the specification of educational objectives. These ideas were later applied, by Ralph Tyler, to the realms of test construction when he was faced with the unscientific diagnostic tests used in the biological sciences at Ohio University. He was in favour of having teachers:

> formulate the course objectives, define the objectives in terms of student behaviour, collect situations in which students are to indicate the presence or absence of each objective, and provide the method of evaluating the student's reactions in the light of each objective. (Tyler, 1932)

Tyler was, in effect, proposing an early description of what was later to be called 'criterion reference' testing (see Chapter 4). He went on, in his classic text 'Basic Principles of Curriculum and Instruction' (1949), to detail a series of techniques by which 'materials are selected, content is outlined, instructional procedures are developed and tests and examinations are prepared.' And, as a first step in the systematic and intelligent study of educational programmes, he suggests that 'we must be sure as to the educational objectives aimed at' (1949, p.3). The objectives are not to be confused with things which the instructor is to do, they must be expressed in terms of changes in student behaviour:

> Since the real purpose of education is not to have the instructor perform certain activities but to bring about significant changes in the students' patterns of behaviour, it becomes important to recognize that any

> statement of the objectives of the school should be a statement of changes to take place in students. (Tyler, 1949, p.44)

He claims that the most useful form for stating objectives is to include both the kind of behaviour to be developed in the student and 'the content or area of life in which this behaviour is to operate' (p.46). The objectives 'to write clear and well-organized reports of social studies projects', 'familiarity with dependable sources of information on questions relating to nutrition' and 'to develop an appreciation of the modern novel', are given by Tyler as models of clear objectives including both behavioural and content aspects, although he does acknowledge that 'to develop an appreciation' may require some further definition.

The 'behavioural objectives' must be defined clearly because they will form the basis for the evaluation procedures, which are an integral part of Tyler's scheme. Choosing and formulating educational objectives and the learning experiences do not complete the planning cycle for Tyler. Evaluation does this because it 'becomes a process for finding out how far the learning experiences as developed and organized are actually producing the desired results' (p.105). There are two aspects to evaluation. The first implies that evaluation must look at the behaviour of the student, and the changes in behaviour as a result of the process of education. The second implies that evaluation must involve more than a single appraisal. At least, it must consist of both an assessment at the beginning of the course of instruction and an appraisal at the end of the programme in order to determine the changes which have taken place. This is not enough for Tyler who expresses a desire for more testing during the educational programme in order to determine the changes in behaviour step by step. His suggestion finds fertile ground in later years in the form of summative and formative testing.

Mager's Behavioural Objectives

While Tyler advocated the use of objectives in the context of evaluation procedures Bloom and his colleagues concentrated on the precise specification of educational objectives without such an emphasis. It was taken up again in 1962, with the accelerating interest being shown in the programmed learning movement, when Robert Mager published a short book aimed at helping instructors to answer the question 'What is worth teaching?' by demonstrating the steps involved in 'Preparing Instructional Objectives.' Mager claimed that, having read the book:

> Given any objective in a subject area with which you are familiar, in all instances be able to identify (label) correctly the performance, the conditions, and the criterion of acceptable performance, when any or all those characteristics are present. (Mager, 1962/1975, p.3)

This statement presents an immediate outline of the three essential components in a Mager objective: first, the behaviour or performance to be accepted as evidence that the learner has changed; second, the conditions under which the behaviour will be demonstrated; and third, the standards or criteria of acceptable performance against which the success or failure of the learner will be judged. Davies (1976) is correct in assuming that the first component in Mager's scheme includes both of Tyler's dimensions for an objective, the kind of behaviour and the content area. The third incorporates Tyler's demand for evaluation as part of the complete cycle. Thus, Mager is taking on board that aspect explicitly excluded in Bloom's Taxonomy, and as such can be seen as a major advance in the application of behavioural objectives.

In one of the asides in his book (it was a scrambled programmed text, with 'optional material' scattered throughout, which the reader could 'save for a rainy day') he vividly describes what can happen when objectives are not stated clearly. It concerns students who were learning how to operate and repair a large, complex electronic system. The course goal was 'to be able to operate and maintain' the system. Time on the actual machine was limited and in order to increase the practice time students were taught in the classroom. The instructor would point out a component on a diagram and ask what effect it would have on the system if it failed. The students traced back through their individual diagrams and listed the symptoms. Of course, this is the exact opposite to what was expected of the operator, who would observe a symptom and then deduce the possible causes. As Mager said, the students were learning to run forwards by being taught to run backwards!

The correct approach was demonstrated in his analysis of the separate skills and objectives required by the general statement that students were 'able to read electrical meters.'

> 1. Given a meter scale, be able to identify (state) the value indicated by the position of the pointer as accurately as the construction of the meter will allow.
> 2. Be able to identify (state) the value indicated by the pointer on meter scales that are linear, non-linear, reversed, or bi-directional.

> 3. Given a meter with a single scale and a range switch, be able to identify (state) the value indicated by the pointer for each of the ranges shown by the range switch.
> 4. Given a meter with several scales and a range switch, be able to identify (state) the scale corresponding to each setting of the range switch.
> (Mager, 1962/75, p.53)

There are improvements that can still be made to these objectives, for example, by adding to the criterion for reading the value in objective 1. The objectives can also be made too specific and in doing so may lose their value. Adding lighting and room temperature conditions to the objective 'will type a specimen letter, in accordance with office procedures, on an IBM PC word-processor and obtain one paper copy, with no mistakes, in less than five minutes', will not add a great deal to the usefulness of the objective. Adding details of the type of software running on the machine or the type of printer or even paper (single sheet, continuous roll) will improve its value.

In answering the performance question 'What should the learner be able to do?' Mager suggests that action verbs are going to be more useful than 'fuzzies' or words open to a wide range of interpretation. 'Fuzzies' include such words as: to know, to understand, to <u>really</u> understand, to <u>fully</u> appreciate, to grasp the significance of. The action words open to fewer interpretations include: to write, to recite, to construct, to solve.

The conditions under which the performance will be demonstrated should clarify what the student brings to the situation and what is provided. Mager suggests a number of examples: given any reference of the learner's choice... ; given a standard set of tools... ; without the aid of a slide rule.... Thus, the statement 'be able to solve problems in algebra' is changed to something along the lines 'given a linear algebraic equation be able to solve (write the solution) for the unknown without the aid of references, tables, or calculating devices.'

Finally, the criterion must be made explicit because:

> if we can specify the acceptable performance for each objective, we will have a standard against which to test our instruction; we will have the means for determining whether our instruction is successful in achieving our instructional intent. If, for example, our best experience and wisdom tell us that we must not consider a student competent until that student can perform within a strict time limit, then we know that we will

> have to instruct and assist that student until the desired performance level is reached. (Mager, 1962/1975, p.71)

For Mager the criterion is essentially a measure of the correctness of instruction for a particular student. When the student fails to reach the required level, the instruction is failing as well as the student. The criterion should not be a minimum or barely tolerable criterion, it should describe the desirable performance, although this will depend on the specific circumstances, as Mager says, it may be acceptable for a shipping clerk to occasionally tie a knot that slips, but that level of performance would not be acceptable for a surgeon. The criterion can be expressed as speed, accuracy or quality. A speed criterion is usually given as a time limit within which the performance must occur and accuracy usually indicates the limits eg. be able to tell the time shown on a clock to within one minute. Quality may be reduced to descriptions of accuracy, or it may include a quantitative specification eg. the number of examples to be given in a definition.

Mager's contribution to the development of specific behavioural objectives has been perfectly summarized by Davies:

> Rarely during the history of education has such a small book (62 pages), with so much blank paper, been as influential on both the thinking and practice, loves and fears of both British and American teachers. (Davies, 1976, p.57)

Objectives and the Principles of Instructional Design

Objectives have continued to occupy a central role in systems of instructional design and the components of operational definitions of objectives have been further extended by Gagné and Briggs (1979) from three to five, although they are not widely different from those of Mager and do not 'differ from them in any crucial respect.' Rather, there are differences in emphasis and distinctions which previously had not been highlighted, in particular, the distinction between verbs for 'action' and verbs used to identify the 'learned capability' implied by the behaviour under observation. There are five components in the scheme: action, object, situation, tools and constraints, and capability to be learned. The example of the poor objective 'types a letter' is used by Gagné and Briggs to illustrate the five components.

1. **ACTION.** The objective is fine with respect to the action component.
2. **OBJECT.** The object of the performance is clear ie. a letter is to be produced.
3. **SITUATION.** Clearly this requires some improvement: is she given a letter written in long hand to type, or is it on a tape, or even in note from?
4. **TOOLS AND OTHER CONSTRAINTS.** This aspect needs to be developed. What sort of typewriter is to be used, is a carbon required, what is the length of the letter? Obviously, different limits will be set for students at different levels.
5. **CAPABILITY TO BE LEARNED.** 'Types a letter' does not say much about the different human capabilities that may be involved in the process of producing the letter. It could mean that the letter is to be copied, or it could be that the letter is to be composed. These will require very different capabilities.

The poor objective is up-graded along the following lines: given a letter inquiring about the shipping of an order (situation) the student will generate (the learned capability, implying a problem-solving approach) a letter in reply (object) by typing (action), using an electric typewriter, making one carbon of a one-page letter (tools and other constraints).

Hierarchies, Capabilities and Systems

The new component 'capability to be learned' is related to Gagné's hierarchy of learning categories (Figure 3-3) which originally arranged learning into eight different types ranging from the simple to the complex. The most important class of conditions that distinguished one type from another in the hierarchy was the initial state of each. Gagné (1965) called this its prerequisites. At the higher end of the hierarchy each type has the previous types as prerequisites.

The arrangement of these different types of learning into a hierarchical structure reflects Gagné's behaviouristic S-R origins, which became less relevant with the rise of more sophisticated models of human cognition, particularly the information processing model which he later adopted. Gagné acknowledges this change in emphasis in his preface to the third edition of 'The Conditions of Learning':

> The considerable shift in orientation from its previous edition requires a very different organisation for this

Figure 3-3. Gagné's Hierarchy of Learning Types, based on Conditions of Learning (1965, First Edition).

Type 8. Problem solving, requires the internal events usually called thinking, which requires as prerequisites:

Type 7. Principle or rule learning, is the forming a chain of two or more concepts, which requires as prerequisites:

Type 6. Concept learning, requires a response that identifies an entire class of objects or events, which has as prerequisites:

Type 5. Multiple discriminations, requires different responses to similar stimuli, which has as prerequisites Type 4 or Type 3.

Type 4. Verbal association or the learning of chains that are verbal, which has as prerequisite Type 2.

Type 3. Chaining of 2 or more S-R connections, which has as prerequisite Type 2.

Type 2. Stimulus-response learning, as found in the work of Thorndike and Skinner, which Gagné felt did not have Type 1 as a prerequisite.

Type 1. Signal learning, the classical conditioning of Pavlov, the most basic type of learning.

> one, and has occasioned its being largely rewritten to include much new material. This book, I feel, deserves a preface which is both frank and more than usually detailed. (Gagné, 1976, p.iv)

The hierarchy of learning types was removed and its place was taken by the 'learned dispositions or capabilities' which form the varieties of learning outcomes. There are now five of these (Gagné, 1985): intellectual skills, cognitive strategies, verbal information, motor skills and attitudes and, unlike the learning types, they do not have 'simply ordered relationships with one another.' Their order of presentation is mainly for convenience. However, the higher levels of the old hierarchy are incorporated into the fabric of the new scheme, while the

Figure 3-4. Verbs Describing Human Capabilities. (Based on Gagné and Briggs, 1979; Gagné, 1985)

CAPABILITY	ASSOCIATED VERB
Intellectual Skill	
Discrimination	DISCRIMINATES
Concrete Concept	IDENTIFIES
Defined Concept	CLASSIFIES
Rule	DEMONSTRATES
Higher-order Rule (Problem Solving)	GENERATES
Cognitive Strategy	ORIGINATES
Verbal Information	STATES
Motor Skill	EXECUTES
Attitude	CHOOSES

lower half of the hierarchy is ultimately relegated to a single category. Type 8, problem solving, becomes associated with both intellectual skills and cognitive strategies capabilities, while Type 7 (principle or rule learning), Type 6 (concept learning) and Type 5 (multiple discrimination) are incorporated in the intellectual skills capability. Each capability has 'standard verbs' associated with it to describe what will be present when the capability is learned (Figure 3-4).

Intellectual skills involve 'knowing how', or procedural knowledge. They include making discriminations, as when a child learns to make the correct sound associated with a given letter, rather than another sound. Identification, the capability verb for concrete concepts, is in evidence when an individual can respond to a collection of things by distinguishing among them and is able to name the individual items. Putting things into a class and responding to any instance of the class as a member of that class is evidence of a defined concept, and the ability to respond to any instance of a class of situations with an appropriate instance of a class of performances is evidence of a rule being used. Gagné (1985) feels that learning of rules is of vast importance because rules make up the bulk of what is learned in schools. One aspect of problem solving is found when the learner discovers a combination of previously learned rules and combines them to generate a solution in a novel situation.

A further aspect of problem solving is associated with the cognitive strategies capability, which is represented by the ways that individuals focus their knowledge and skills on problem situations that may not have been encountered before. Gagné calls these strategies ways of 'using one's head.' The 'problem finding' aspect of cognitive strategies, involving both the identification of novel problems and the translation of known rules into forms which provide the solutions, is of major importance.

Verbal information is also known as declarative knowledge and refers to knowledge that is 'verbalizable.' It can take the form of names or labels, single propositions or facts or collections of meaningfully organised propositions.

Motor skills require the execution of muscular movements, although a more comprehensive term is 'psychomotor' skills because of the necessary co-ordination of bodily systems. The extent of this category can be seen from the examples Gagné (1985) gives, including executing a dive, using a typewriter and adjusting the internal mechanism of a watch.

Learning results in the creation of internal states that influence choices of an individual's action. These outcomes are called attitudes and are made up of three components: a cognitive component, an affective component and a behavioural component. According to Gagné this capability is demonstrated when a person chooses to behave in one manner rather than another.

Gagné and Briggs have attempted to build a framework which takes account of the three areas of educational objectives (cognitive, affective and psychomotor) and integrates them with the various types of learning to form the human capabilities component, thus producing a more coherent scheme.

The addition of this may be seen as an improvement, but there is one glaring omission; the criterion component does not appear in the scheme. There is no mention of the number of mistakes permitted nor the time limit for completion of the job. Gagné and Briggs take issue with Mager on this point:

> Instructional objectives describe the class of performances that may be used to determine whether the implied human capability has been learned. However, they do not state in quantitative terms what criteria will be used to judge whether any particular performance class has been learned.
> (Gagné and Briggs, 1979, p.127)

Two reasons are given for this. First, the criteria should be linked to the different types of human capabilities. Second, criteria of performance are related to the techniques of performance assessment, and it could be confusing to become concerned with assessment procedures when objectives are being described. Statements of objectives always imply 'mastery', but the criterion of mastery needs to be separately decided when considering assessment methods. If the proper conditions are provided the frequently used course design criterion of 90 percent of the students achieving 90 percent of objectives is recommended by Briggs and Gagné. This can have the effect of monitoring both student performance and the adequacy of the instruction.

The objectives movement has given rise to what is now known as the 'systems approach' to instructional design, in which educational technology is related to the process of planning, although the term 'systematic approach' is preferred by some authors because of its cyclical nature (MacDonald-Ross, 1973). Rowntree (1982) sees this as consisting of four stages:

1. Identifying purposes, which includes analysing aims, describing the students, determining the objectives and evaluation procedures.
2. Design of learning, during which objectives and subject matter are analysed, learning sequences and strategies are devised, and media, materials and experiences are selected.
3. Evaluation, when the materials are tried out and monitored.
4. Improvement, during which phase the results of the evaluation stage are reviewed and revisions are made of the products of the previous activities.

Gagné and Briggs (1979) have a similar scheme, but the analysis of objectives is separated from the design of measures of learner performances.

This approach to the design of instruction, with its emphasis on the early specification of objectives, is an essential part of the production of programmed instruction and other behaviourally oriented methods of teaching, including Bloom's 'Learning for Mastery' and Keller's 'Personalized System of Instruction.' The success of such systems must be attributable, in part, to this aspect of the design process.

SUPPORT, CRITICISM AND RESEARCH

Instructional objectives attracted widespread criticism and fervent support in equal measure throughout the early years. Popham (1969) reviewed ten reasons which he found to be used by educators to 'escape the practice of stating their objectives behaviourally.' He saw each of the reasons as carrying its own appeal to different sorts of educators, each with its own degree of reasonableness or emotionality, but each being essentially invalid.

To the suggestion that 'trivial learner behaviours are the easiest to operationalize, hence the really important outcomes of education will be under-emphasised', he did acknowledge that too many examples of behavioural objectives dealt with the picayune, especially those following Mager's examples, most of which dealt with the lowest level of Bloom's Taxonomy. But the fact that it was possible to make such behaviours explicit should result in their identification as unworthy of educational effort and hence their elimination.

It was also suggested that pre-specification of explicit goals prevents the teacher from taking advantage of opportunities unexpectedly occurring in the classroom. Popham argued that serendipity is always welcome in the classroom, but 'it should always be justified in terms of its contribution to the learner's attainment of worthwhile objectives', otherwise it may fall into the category of ephemeral entertainment for pupils.

There are other educational outcomes which are as important as changes in pupil behaviour, such as changes in parental attitudes, community values, etc. and to this Popham responded that all such modifications should be justified in terms of their contribution toward the pupils' achievements and the desired changes in their behaviours.

It was also suggested that the emphasis on behaviour which can be objectively and mechanistically measured must result in a de-humanizing approach to education. This view was based on the erroneous views of measurement as exclusively examination-based, which ignore the 'extremely sophisticated ways of securing qualitative as well as quantitative indices of learner performance.'

Another reason for not specifying educational objectives was that it was somehow undemocratic to plan in advance exactly how the learner should behave after instruction. Popham retorted that teachers generally have an idea of how they wish to behave, and they promote these goals with more or less efficiency. In any case, 'if schools were allowing students to "democratically" deviate from societal mandated goals' they would cease to receive society's support.

The fact that teachers do not specify their goals in terms of measurable behaviours and since that is the way of the real world perhaps it is unreasonable to expect such a dramatic change, was given as another reason for avoiding educational objectives. Not so, replied Popham, they may not, but they should because 'The way teaching really is at the moment just isn't good enough.'

Certain subjects were seen to offer more scope for the specification of student behaviours than others. In the fine arts and humanities it would be particularly difficult.

'Tough but not impossible', was Popham's reply, and he gave an example that many students must have sympathized with:

> Any English teacher, for example, will tell you how difficult it is to make a valid judgement of a pupil's essay response. Yet criteria lurk whenever this teacher does make a judgement, and these criteria must be made explicit.
> (Popham, 1969, p.50)

Another reason for not adopting objectives was that if most educational goals were stated precisely, they would be revealed as generally innocuous. Popham acknowledged this potential threat to school people and declared that much of what goes on in the schools is indefensible. If what is happening in schools is trivial, educators should know it and so should those who support it. He called upon teachers to abandon the ploy of 'obfuscation by generality' and clarify what is being done.

'Measurability implies accountability' and as such represents a good reason for many teachers not using the objectives approach. Teachers might actually be judged on their ability to bring about the desired changes, and so they should be, according to Popham.

He sympathized with the final reason, that it is very difficult and time consuming for teachers to generate precise objectives. The answer to this was to reduce the teacher's load to enable her to become a professional decision-maker and not merely a custodian. Alternatively, funds could be diverted to enable objectives to be generated by external agencies, which would produce alternative objectives for all fields and at all grades.

MacDonald-Ross (1973) looked at both the advantages and disadvantages claimed for behavioural objectives. In their favour he concluded that they formed the basis of the only well-worked out method of rational planning in education, encouraging detailed planning and making explicit previously concealed values. They were seen as providing a basis for evaluation and the choice of instructional means, within a self-improving system which achieves internal consistency and the attainment of its initial aims. Objectives act as a medium of communication and can form the basis for individualising instruction.

However, there were certain disadvantages. The most serious were that there was no view as to the origins of objectives and there were no well-defined prescriptions for deriving them. Although it is claimed that behavioural objectives provide the only objective basis for evaluation, MacDonald-Ross felt that they cannot prescribe the validity of test items because they are inherently ambiguous and various items can usually be written for each objective. He

Figure 3-5. Major Objections to Behavioural Objectives, according to MacDonald-Ross (1973)

Major Objections

1. No consistent view exists as to the origins of objectives.
2. In the educational domain no well-defined prescriptions are available for deriving objectives.
3. Weak prescriptions lead to cycling. This can be costly.
4. Lists of behaviours do not adequately represent the structure of knowledge.
5. The use of behavioural objectives implies a poverty-stricken model of student-teacher interaction.
6. The behavioural objectives scheme suffers from many weaknesses of any operational dogma.
7. Objectives do not prescribe the validity of test items.
8. The level of specificity problem has never been solved.

Minor Objections

9. Defining objectives before the event conflicts with voyages of exploration.
10. Advocates do not show how teachers can use objectives to guide unpredictable classroom events.
11. There are an extremely large number of paths through any body of knowledge, thus reducing the effectiveness of objectives in design.
12. In some disciplines criteria can only be applied after the event.
13. Objectives are inherently ambiguous.
14. Objectives do not communicate intent unambiguously, especially to students.
15. Trivial objectives are the easiest to operationalize, and this is a problem.
16. The relevance of goal-referenced models of education can be questioned.

---

also questioned the level of specificity of objectives: just how specific is it necessary to be to define the required behaviours in a course of instruction? He calculated that to move to a level suggested by Mager, if applied to an average educational psychology text, would require 10,000 objectives in a volume of 150,000 words.

A further disadvantage expressed by MacDonald-Ross was the cost involved in the cyclical nature of testing and modifying instruction to attain preset objectives. He supported the common criticism of objectives, that they represent a poverty-sticken view of student-teacher interaction and, at a more philosophical level, agreed with Pask (1972) that lists of behaviours do not adequately represent the structure of knowledge. His views were summarized as a list of 16 objections to objectives, including many that were to be found in Popham's discussion (Figure 3-5).

The Research

It has been suggested that objectives contribute to student successes because they provide a detailed description of precisely what it is that the student must learn during instruction. Duchastel and Merrill (1973) reviewed the evidence accumulated to answer the question: Does communicating behavioural objectives to students facilitate learning? In studies which investigated the straight comparison between students with and students without objectives they concluded that five studies demonstrated a significant effect due to the availability of behavioural objectives, and five found no difference, for tests of immediate retention. For delayed retention the results were also inconclusive.

Melton (1978) points out that a substantial number of researchers have recorded experiments that lend support to the claim that behavioural objectives enhance relevant learning when presented to students, whilst others show no such enhancement. One aspect, explored by Engel (1968), was that students must be aware of the objectives and must read them for there to be a positive effect. The difficulty of the objectives may also be a factor, according to Brown (1970), for if the objectives are extremely difficult the majority of students will fail to master them and it will be difficult to discriminate between the performance of students who do and do not receive the objectives. These and other results led Melton to the conclusion that there were five conditions under which objectives would be ineffective:

1. If students ignore the objectives provided, either because they are unaware of them, or because prior experience suggests that it is not important to take note of them.
2. If the objectives are too general, or too ambiguous, to be of particular assistance.
3. If the objectives are of extreme facility or difficulty. (The structure of readability of instructional material may be closely related to this condition.)
4. If the objectives of particular interest are only a small proportion of those provided to students.

5. If students are conscientious, or so highly motivated, that they achieve the objectives regardless of whether or not they are specified.

(Melton, 1978, p.294)

Although most research had involved the effects of objectives on relevant learning, Melton pointed to the controversy concerning the effects of objectives on incidental learning. Morse and Tillman (1972) had found that behavioural objectives enhanced relevant learning without detracting from incidental learning against unspecified objectives. Whereas, Duchastel (1972, 1977) demonstrated that providing objectives had a detrimental effect on incidental learning. Confounding these observations, Rothkopf and Kaplan (1972, 1974) found the provision of behavioural objectives enhanced both relevant and incidental learning. Melton reasoned from the experimental details in these studies that the effect of the objectives will depend on when they are presented to the student and how they are used during study. When objectives are given prior to study and are read by the students before commencing their study the objectives would act as orienting stimuli, enhancing relevant learning but depressing incidental learning. Objectives read after the period of study would act as reinforcing stimuli, enhancing relevant learning but not at the expense of incidental learning.

When the interaction of objectives and the type of learning was investigated only one study out of seven found objectives to be more effective with one type of learning (knowledge) than with others, and this was not sustained on the retention test.

When learner characteristics were considered, there was some evidence of interactions between such characteristics and provision of objectives, with middle ability students benefitting more from objectives than either high or low ability students. Kueter (1970) found behavioural objectives to be less effective for personality traits of submissiveness, self-control, considerateness, conscientiousness, or low ergic tension. Objectives appear to reduce the level of anxiety for some students (Merrill and Towle, 1971).

Investigations of the hypothesis that students who receive objectives will take less time in learning were few but two demonstrated a great reduction in learning time if the learners had control over how and when they learned. Mager and Clark (1963) reported a reduction in training time of 65 percent, with the learners being better equipped than graduates of the traditional course. Learners were provided with 24 pages of detailed objectives, classes were cancelled and the students were told that they would have complete control over their learning and could ask for instruction when they required it. In a further experiment a saving of 50 percent in learning time was observed. Smith (1970), in a more controlled experiment, did not support previous findings and Duchastel and Merrill caution that studies reported by Mager and Clark are heavily confounded by the student control variable.

Although the research has demonstrated some benefits for courses in which objectives are specified for the benefit of both students and teachers, it must be remembered that the specification of objectives is usually one part of what is now known as the 'systems approach' to course design. Evaluations of the benefits of objectives in isolation can only measure the effects of one of several components, whereas the basis of the systems approach is its synergism. As such, it makes sense to evaluate the total system, as well as the contributions of the individual parts. The programmed instruction 'system', which gave the initial impetus for behavioural objectives, was discussed in the previous chapter. In the following chapter the major mastery 'systems' will be evaluated.

REFERENCES

Block, J.H. (1971) Mastery Learning. London: Holt, Rinehart and Winston.

Bloom, B.S. et al. (1956) Taxonomy of Educational Objectives Handbook I: Cognitive Domain. N.Y.: McKay.

Bloom, B.S. (1968/81) 'Learning for Mastery', (UCLA-CSEIP) The Evaluation Comment, 1(2). In B.S. Bloom (Ed) All Our Children Learning. London: McGraw-Hill.

Bobbitt, F. (1924) How To Make a Curriculum. Boston: Houghton Mifflin.

Brown, J.L. (1970) 'The Effects of Revealing Instructional Objectives on the Learning of Political Concepts and Attitudes in Two Role-playing Games.' Unpublished Doctoral dissertation, University of California, Los Angeles.

Charters, W.W. (1924) Curriculum Construction, N.Y.: MacMillan.

Davies, I.K. (1976) Objectives in Curriculum Design. London: McGraw-Hill.

Duchastel, P.C. (1972) Incidental and Relevant Learning with Instructional Objectives: Technical Memo 66. Tallahassee: Florida State University, CAI Centre.

Duchastel, P.C. (1977) Functions of Instructional Objectives: Organization and Direction. Paper presented at the meeting of the American Educational Research Association, New York, April.

Duchastel, P.C. and Merrill, P.F. (1973) 'The effects of behavioural objectives on learning: a review of empirical studies', Review of Educational Research, 43(1), 53-69.

Engel, R.S. (1968) 'An Experimental Study of the Effect of Stated Behavioural Objectives on Achievement in a Unit of Instruction on Negative and Rational Base Systems of Numeration.' Unpublished Master's thesis, University of Maryland, College Park.

Furst, E.J. (1981) 'Bloom's taxonomy of educational objectives for the cognitive domain: philosophical and educational issues', Review of Educational Research, 51(4), 441-453.

Gagné, R.M. (1965) The Conditions of Learning. (1st Edition) London: Holt, Rinehart and Winston.

Gagné, R.M. (1976) The Conditions of Learning. (2nd Edition) London: Holt, Rinehart and Winston.

Gagné, R.M. (1985) The Conditions of Learning. (4th Edition) London: Holt, Rinehart and Winston.

Gagné, R.M. and Briggs, L.J. (1979) Principles of Instructional Design. (2nd Edition) London: Holt, Rinehart and Winston.

Gagné, R.M. and Paradise, N.E. (1961) 'Abilities and learning sets in knowledge acquisition', Psychological Monographs, 75(14), Whole No. 518.

Green, T.F. (1964) 'Teaching, acting and behaving', Harvard Educational Review, 34, 507-524,

Herbart, J.F. (1924) The Science of Education, London: Routledge and Kegan Paul.

Harrow, A.J. (1972) A Taxonomy of the Psychomotor Domain. N.Y.: McKay.

Keller, F.S. (1968) 'Goodbye, Teacher', Journal of Applied Behaviour Analysis', 1, 79-87.

Krathwohl, D.R., Bloom, B.S. and Masia, B.B. (1964) Taxonomy of Educational Objectives Handbook II: Affective Domain. N.Y.: McKay.

Kropp, R.P and Stoker, H.W. (1966) The Construction and Validation of Tests of the Cognitive Processes Described in The Taxonomy of Educational Objectives. Washington, D.C.: U.S. Office of Education.

Kueter, R.A. (1970) 'Instructional Strategies: The Effect of Personality Factors on Recognition Learning Using Statements of Behavioural Objectives as Opposed to No Statements of Behavioural Objectives Prior to Learning.' Unpublished Doctoral dissertation, Indiana University.

MacDonald-Ross, M. (1973) 'Behavioural Objectives: A Critical Review', Instructional Science, 2, 1-52.

Madaus, G.F., Woods, E.M. and Nuttall, R.L. (1973) 'A causal model analysis of Bloom's taxonomy', American Educational Research Journal, 10, 253-262.

Mager, R.F. (1962/75) Preparing Instructional Objectives. Belmont: Pitman Learning.

Mager, R.F and Clark, C. (1963) 'Explorations in student controlled instruction', Psychological Reports, 13, 71-76.

Melton, R.F. (1978) 'Resolution of conflicting claims concerning the effect of behavioural objectives on student learning', Review of Educational Research, 48(2), 291-302.

Merrill, P.F. and Towle, N.J. (1971) 'Interaction of abilities and anxiety with availability of objectives and/or test items on computer-based task performance', Proceedings of the 79th Annual Convention, American Psychological Association, 539-540.

Morse, J.A. and Tillman, M.H. (1972) Effects on Achievement Of Possession of Behavioural Objectives and Training Concerning Their Use. Paper presented at the meeting of the American Educational Research Association, Chicago.

Ormell, C.P. (1974) 'Bloom's taxonomy and the objectives of education', Educational Research, 17, 3-18.

Ormell, C.P. (1979) 'The problem of analysing understanding', Educational Research, 22, 32-38.

Pask, G. (1972) 'A fresh look at cognition and the individual', International Journal of Man-Machine Studies, 4, 211-216.

Popham, J.W. (1969) 'Objectives and instruction'. In W.J. Popham, E.W. Eisner, H.J. Sullivan and L.L. Tyler (Eds) Instructional Objectives. Chicago: Rand McNally.

Pring, R. (1971) 'Bloom's taxonomy: a philosophical critique (2)', Cambridge Journal of Education, 1, 83-91.

Rothkopf, E.Z. and Kaplan, R. (1972) 'Exploration of the effect of density and specificity of instructional objectives on learning from text', Journal of Educational Psychology, 63, 295-302.

Rothkopf, E.Z. and Kaplan, R. (1974) 'Instructional objectives as directions to learners: effect of passage length and amount of objective-relevant content', Journal of Educational Psychology, 4, 448-456.

Rowntree, D. (1982) Educational Technology in Curriculum Development. London: Harper and Row.

Seddon, G.M. (1978) 'The properties of Bloom's taxonomy of educational objectives for the cognitive domain', Review of Educational Research, 48, 303-323.

Simpson, E.J. (1966) The Classification of Educational Objectives: Psychomotor Domain. University of Illinois, Research Project No.: OE 5-85-104.

Smith, J.M. (1970) 'Relations among Behavioural Objectives, Time of Acquisition, and Retention.' Unpublished Doctoral dissertation, University of Maryland.

Sockett, H. (1971) 'Bloom's taxonomy: a philosophical critique (1)', Cambridge Journal of Education, 1, 16-25.

Spencer, H. (1910) Education: Intellectual, Moral and Physical, London: Appleton.
Travers, R.M.W. (1980) 'Taxonomies of educational objectives and theories of classification', Educational Evaluation and Policy Analysis, 2, 5-23.
Tyler, R.W. (1932) 'The construction of examinations in botany and zoology', Service Studies in Higher Education, Ohio State University, Bureau of Educational Research Monographs, 15, 49-50.
Tyler, R.W. (1949) Basic Principles of Curriculum and Instruction. Chicago: University of Chicago Press.

CHAPTER 4

MASTERING LEARNING

Although early attempts at developing a scientific approach to learning were not always as successful as their proponents anticipated, they have led to an approach to learning that does produce consistent benefits in terms of achievement, benefits that are educationally significant.

Mastery learning is embodied in Bloom's (1968) 'Learning For Mastery' and Keller's (1968) 'Personalized System of Instruction.' Bloom's approach was developed to exploit mastery learning in the schoolroom, whereas Keller developed his system for higher education. However, both have been applied in many different contexts and have been found to be very powerful methods for increasing student performance in a wide range of activities.

BLOOM'S LEARNING FOR MASTERY

Bloom (1968) indicated that a learning strategy for mastery may be derived from the work of Carroll (1963), with support from the ideas of Morrison (1926), Skinner (1954) and Bruner (1966). Block (1971) traces the influences back to Washburne's (1922) Winnetka Plan and Morrison's approach at the University of Chicago's Laboratory School of 1926. In both systems mastery was defined in terms of particular educational objectives and mastery of each unit was required of students before they proceeded to the next unit. An ungraded diagnostic-progress test was administered at the completion of each unit to provide feedback on the adequacy of the student's learning. The test either indicated mastery, usually set at a level of 80-90%, or it highlighted the material the student still had to master. On the basis of the results of the diagnostic test each student's original instruction could be supplemented with appropriate remedial materials so that he could complete his unit, by obtaining a score reaching the mastery criterion. Although popular well into the 1930's these ideas eventually disappeared due primarily to a lack of the technology to sustain them (Block, 1971). They didn't emerge again until the late 1950's and 1960's, as a corollary of programmed instruction. The basic idea underlying programmed instruction being that the learning of any behaviour, no matter how complex, rested upon the learning of a sequence of less complex component behaviours. Theoretically, by breaking down complex behaviour into a chain of component parts and by ensuring mastery of every link in the chain, it would be possible for any student to master even the most complex skills.

The research in programmed instruction showed that it worked very well for some students, especially those requiring small steps, drill and frequent reinforcement, but it was not so effective for all students, and it did not provide a useful mastery model in itself.

Bloom (1968) based his 'Learning For Mastery' (LFM) on the model proposed by J. Carroll (1963). This requires 'that the task can be unequivocally described and that means can be found for making valid judgement as to when the learner has accomplished the learning task - that is, has achieved the learning goal which has been set for him.'

A Model of School Learning

Carroll made the assumption that the work of the school can be broken down into a series of learning tasks. Although he admitted that this can be called into question because, in the school, the various tasks to be learned are not necessarily treated as being separate and distinct, and the process of teaching is often organised so that learning will take place 'incidentally' and in the course of other activities.

Some activities are not included as being appropriate for the model of learning that Carroll has in mind. For example, it is not intended to apply to those goals of the school which do not lend themselves to being considered as learning tasks, such as those having to do with attitudes and dispositions.

The model says that the learner will succeed in learning a given task to the extent that he spends the amount of time that he needs to learn the task. 'Spending time' means actually spending time on the act of learning. It is not 'elapsed time', but the time during which the person is oriented to the learning task and actively engaged in learning.

The variables in the model are considered under two headings: 1) determinants of time needed for learning, and 2) determinants of time spent in learning.

Time Needed in Learning

There are three factors affecting the time needed in learning, according to Carroll: Aptitude, Quality of Instruction, and Ability to Understand Instruction.

1. Aptitude

Common experience, as well as abundant research evidence, suggests that the amounts of time needed by the children even under ideal conditions will differ widely. Carroll suggests that the amount of time each pupil will need to learn a task under optimal conditions is the primary measure of a variable he calls 'aptitude for learning this task.' Learners who need only a small amount of time are said to have high aptitude; learners who need a large amount of time are said to have low aptitude. Some learners, Carroll admits, will never learn even under these optimal conditions; and these learners would need an indefinitely large (or an infinite) amount of time to learn the task.

The measure of aptitude is specific to the task under consideration. It may be regarded as a function of numerous other variables, such as the amount of prior learning or it may also depend upon a series of traits or characteristics of the learner which enter into a wide variety of tasks. These traits may be accounted for solely on the basis of generalized prior learnings, or they may reflect genetically determined individual characteristics.

Bloom (1968) contrasts this view with a common view that high levels of achievement are possible only for the most able students. Implicit in Carroll's formulation is the idea that all students can achieve mastery of a given task if they are provided with sufficient time. Therefore, mastery is available to all, if the right means can be found to help each individual. Bloom quotes evidence to support this, based on the grade norms for many standardized achievement tests. Such norms show that certain scores attained by the most able students at one grade level are achieved by the majority of students at a later grade.

Bloom believes that there is likely to be a small percentage of students (1%-5%), with special talents for a given subject, who are able to learn and use a subject with greater fluency than other students. These may be inherited, or may be developed by special training or interests. There is another small percentage of individuals who have extreme difficulty in learning particular subjects. Between these extremes are approximately 90% of the individuals for whom, Carroll and Bloom believe, aptitudes are predictive of rate of learning rather than the level or complexity of learning that is possible.

This means that 95% of students are capable of learning a subject to a high level of mastery, with up to 95% of a class being capable of attaining the equivalent of an A-grade, previously associated with the top 5-10%. Bloom assumes that for some students more time, effort and help may be required to reach this level, and for some the time and help required may make such achievement prohibitive.

Thus, a major problem for mastery-learning strategists is to find a way of reducing the time and effort that the less able students are required to make, to a point where it is not prohibitive. Bloom points out that students' aptitudes can be changed by appropriate learning experiences in the school and in the home, and that such changes can be most effectively brought about in the elementary years of schooling and during the early years in the home. Even if such changes cannot be effected in the early years it is highly probable that more effective learning conditions can reduce the amount of time required for learning to mastery.

2. Quality of Instruction

Carroll states that one job of the teacher is to organize and present the task to be learned in such a way that the learner can learn it as rapidly and as efficiently as he is able. This means that the learner must be put into adequate sensory contact with the material to be learned and that the various aspects of the learning task must be presented in such an order and with such detail that every step of the learning is adequately prepared for by a previous step. It may also mean that the instruction must be adapted for the special needs and characteristics of the learner, including his stage of learning. This variable applies not only to the performance of a teacher but also to the characteristics of textbooks, workbooks, films, and teaching programmes.

If the quality of instruction is anything less than optimal, it is probable that the learner will need more time to learn the task than he would otherwise need, although some learners will be more handicapped by poor instruction than others.

Bloom (1968) is concerned that we have fallen into the trap of looking at the class of 30 or so students and asking the questions 'What is the best teacher for the group?'; 'What is the best method of instruction for the group?'; 'What is the best instructional material for the group?' He maintains that it is necessary to start from a very different perspective in which each individual student may require very different types and qualities of instruction. In other words 'the same content and objectives of instruction may be learned by different students as the result of very different types of instruction.' For example, some students may need more examples, some may require more approval or reinforcement, or more concrete illustrations or explanations.

The example of home tutoring of middle-class students is quoted by Bloom to illustrate the benefits of the quality of instruction suited to the student's needs. A third of the middle-class students in one study received home tuition in algebra when parents saw the school as failing to provide the necessary tuition. These students received relatively high grades for algebra, with the relationship between mathematics aptitude tests at the start of the course and their achievement at the end of the year being almost zero. With no extra tuition the relationship between aptitude and achievement was highly correlated (+0.9).

3. Ability to Understand Instruction

A further factor affecting the time needed in learning is the ability to understand instruction. Carroll suggests that this variable interacts with the method of instruction in a special and interesting way. It could be measured as some combination of 'general intelligence' and 'verbal ability'; the former of these two would come into play 'in instructional situations where the learner is left to infer for himself the concepts and relationships inherent in the material to be learned', while the latter would come into play 'whenever the instruction utilized language beyond the grasp of the learner.'

Bloom comments that in schools there is frequently a single teacher and a single set of instructional materials for all students in a given class. The student who has facility in understanding the teacher's communications has little difficulty in learning the subject. However, the student with the same basic aptitude for the subject but lacking the ability to understand the teacher or the text will experience considerable difficulty in learning.

This is the point at which the student's abilities interact with the instructional materials. For Bloom this ability will primarily be determined by verbal ability and reading comprehension because schools place such great stress on these abilities.

Bloom (1964) in 'Stability and Change in Human Characteristics' presents evidence that it is possible to produce changes in verbal ability early in life by appropriate training, but that such changes are more difficult later on in life, although vocabulary and reading ability may be improved to some extent at all ages. Therefore, the greatest immediate pay-off in this area will come from modifications in the instruction. Bloom suggests that given help and various types of aids, individual teachers can find ways of modifying their instruction to fit the differing needs of their students. He gives examples of how to overcome this problem within the school context:

1) Group Study: Small groups of students meeting regularly to go over points of difficulty were found to

be most effective, especially if this could be arranged in a non-competitive atmosphere, with more able students being provided with opportunities to strengthen their understanding while helping less able students to grasp ideas presented through alternative ways of explanation.

2) Tutorial Help: This is very costly, but should be made available to students as they require it, especially where difficulties cannot be corrected in any other way.

3) Text Books: The provision of various text books providing instruction for different abilities, rather than adopting one set book, can obviously be of benefit.

4) Workbooks and Programmed Texts: Drill and practice or small steps with frequent reinforcement may help some students and programmed texts or workbooks can provide these.

5) Audio-visual Methods and Academic Games: Bloom suggests that some students may learn a particular idea from concrete illustrations and vivid explanations which AV methods (video tapes, filmstrips etc.) can provide. Other students may require direct laboratory experiences, games and computer simulations. In other words the highest priority need not always be given to abstract and verbal ways of instruction. The suggestion is not for particular materials to be used by particular students throughout the course, but for such materials as are appropriate to be used in helping students to overcome their difficulties.

Time Spent in Learning

In Carroll's model there are two factors which directly affect the time which the student actually spends in learning.

1. Time Allowed for Learning or 'Opportunity'

This is the first factor in the time actually spent in learning. Carroll comments that schools may allow less than adequate time for many students learning many tasks. Schools respond to differences in learning rates in many ways, in particular, they ignore these differences; a certain amount of time is provided for everybody to learn, and no more. At the other extreme is the case where each student is allowed to proceed exactly at his own rate; private instruction in music or foreign languages and self-instruction by teaching-machine or other means are approximations to this case. The middle position is occupied by learning situations in which there is some kind of 'ability grouping.'

Obviously, failure to allow enough time for learning produces incomplete learning. If a person needs two hours to learn something and is allowed only one hour, and if we assume that learning proceeds linearly with time, the degree of learning is only 50%. Carroll feels that one of the most aversive things which a school can do is not to allow sufficient time for a well-motivated child to master a given learning task before the next step is taken up. Children meet such frustrations by indifference or the more extreme avoidance reactions and are, in any case, handicapped in undertaking the next task.

This is the key to mastery. Aptitude and other factors determine the rate of learning and all students can achieve mastery if they devote the amount of time needed, and for this they must be provided with sufficient time.

However, it is not just the amount of time that accounts for the level of achievement, but the amount of time in relation to other factors such as quality of instruction, aptitude and verbal ability and also the student's ability to persevere with the task in hand.

2. Perseverance

The second factor is the amount of time the learner is willing to spend in the learning process. Carroll describes this as consisting of three attitudes: (1) a marked willingness to spend time beyond the ordinary schedule, in a given task; (2) a willingness to withstand discomfort, which includes adjusting to shortened lunch hours, or no lunch hours, working without holidays and withstanding fatigue; (3) a willingness to face failure, which brings with it a realization that patient work may lead to successful termination of the task in hand.

A learner who needs a certain amount of time to learn a task may or may not be willing to persevere for that amount of time in trying to learn. The learner may not be motivated to learn at all, or may regard the task as something too difficult for him to learn; in either case, he may spend no time at all in trying to learn. He may, of course, be so highly motivated that he would be willing to spend more time than he needs in order to reach a specified criterion of mastery.

This variable, if it is not sufficiently great to allow the learner to attain mastery, operates in the conceptual model to reduce the degree of learning. It is a function partly of 'motivation' or the desire to learn and may also be a function of what are ordinarily called emotional variables. For example, one may desire to learn but be unable to endure frustrations caused by difficulties in the learning task.

Students approach different tasks with different degrees of perseverance and, if frustrated in learning, will reduce the time devoted to a subject. Bloom suggests that it may be difficult to manipulate the perseverance of a student and that changes in the type of instruction and learning materials may help students to master material for a given level of perseverance. Then, as a corollary of this action, the reward and perceived success can raise the student's level of perseverance. As students attain mastery they are likely to raise their level of perseverance in related areas.

Bloom found that with appropriate instructional resources the demands for perseverance may be reduced. Frequent feedback accompanied by specific help in instruction and materials can reduce not only the time taken but also the perseverance required. Improvement in the quality of instruction (explanations, illustrations, etc.) may also reduce the required perseverance. He concludes that:

> There seems to be little reason to make learning so difficult that only a small proportion of the students can persevere to mastery. Endurance and unusual perseverance may be appropriate for long-distance running - they are not great virtues in their own right. The emphasis should be on learning, not vague ideas of discipline and endurance. (Bloom, 1968/81, p.164)

Thus, the model involves five elements - three residing in the individual and two stemming from external conditions. Factors in the individual are (1) aptitude - the amount of time needed to learn the task under optimal conditions, (2) ability to understand instruction, and (3) perseverance - the amount of time the learner is willing to engage actively in learning. Factors in external conditions are (4) opportunity - the time allowed for learning, and (5) the quality of instruction - a measure of the degree to which instruction is presented so that it will not require additional time for mastery beyond that required in view of aptitude.

Assessment Criteria

Carroll's model advocates a 'criterion referenced' assessment procedure, as suggested by Tyler (1932), in which the student's performance is judged according to how well he has done by comparison with some predetermined criterion. This contrasts with the traditional 'norm referenced' assessment in which a given student is judged against the performance of his colleagues.

Criterion referenced tests provide a standard against which all student performances can be measured, and can ensure a minimum standard of competence. The driving test is a good example of this kind of assessment: all learners take the test and if they don't reach the criterion level they fail but may repeat the test until they reach the set level of competence. Norm referencing of a group at a driving school may result in a good distribution of grades from fail to A-grade, but this would not necessarily mean that even the A-grade students were able to reach the criterion level. It would mean that they could out-perform their colleagues, but the overall standard could still be below that required for safe driving on the highway.

The programmed learning movement popularized criterion referencing, with the programme writer producing a criterion test related to the objectives of his programme. The aim of the programme was to teach in such a way that 90% of the students obtained 90% on the criterion test. To attain this the programme writer would test the programme and revise areas of the text which produced low scores in the test. He would have to:

> resist the pressure from psychometricians who have had him insert some extra-hard questions and cut out easy ones - 'in order to spread students out a bit and show that some have achieved more than others.' He would reply, 'No, my intention is not to show whether some have learned more than others but to sow whether or not they have learned well enough to have attained the objectives. If all score 100% I shall be well pleased.' (Rowntree, 1977, p.180)

With norm referenced tests the aim is to produce the sort of achievement distribution shown in Figure 4-1, whereas the criterion referenced test should produce the achievement results shown in Figure 4-2.

Bloom (1968) took these ideas and transformed Carroll's conceptual model into an effective working model for mastery. He argued that if aptitudes were predictive of the <u>rate</u> at which (and not the <u>level to</u> which) a student could learn a given task, then it should be possible to fix the degree of learning expected of students at some level of mastery and to systematically manipulate the variables in Carroll's model so that all or almost all students attained it. He also reasoned that if aptitude for a subject was normally distributed in the student population and they were provided with uniform instruction in terms of quality and

Figure 4-1. Aptitude-Achievement for Uniform Instruction per Learner.

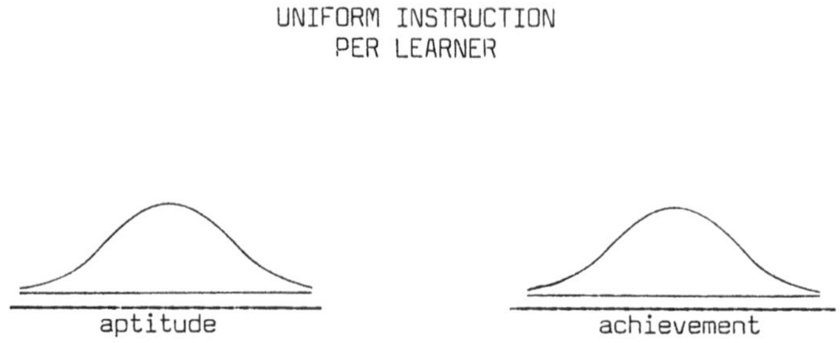

learning time, then achievement on completion of instruction would be normally distributed (Figure 4-1).

However, if the learner were to receive optimal quality of instruction and learning time then a majority of students could expect to attain mastery and there would be little or no relationship between aptitude and achievement (Figure 4-2).

Learning Hierarchies

Bloom also incorporated Gagné's theory of learning hierarchies in his learning for mastery approach. This theory states that the learning of any intellectual skill is important because it supports the learning of more complex skills. The support is only there if the previously learned skills are readily available when the new learning is taking place. Gagné suggests that mastery means 'readily accessible to recall at the time of learning of the more complex skill.'

Learning hierarchy research started with Gagné's early work with programmed learning of mathematical skills. In the first investigation a programmed book was used to teach a hierarchy of twenty-two elements leading to the ability to solve linear equations. Gagné felt that each element in the hierarchy could not be acquired unless the learners possessed those prerequisite skills found at lower levels in the hierarchy. These prerequisites could be determined by asking 'What would the individual have to be able to do in order that he can attain successful performance on this task, provided he is given only instructions?' (Gagné, 1962, p.358). He proposed that transfer from one learning set to another standing above it in the hierarchy will be zero if the lower one cannot be recalled, and will be as much as

Figure 4-2. Aptitude-Achievement for Optimal Instruction per Learner.

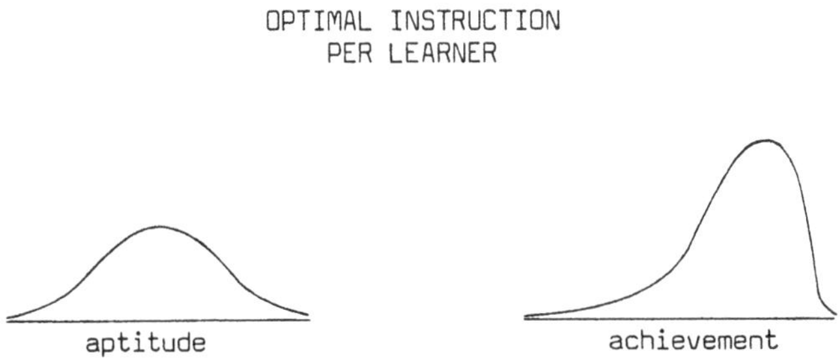

100% if it can be recalled. From this it follows that attaining each new learning set is dependent on recall of previous subordinate sets interacting with the effects of instructions.

> In order for learning to occur at any point in the hierarchy, according to this theory, each of the learning sets subordinate to a given task must be highly recallable, and integrated by a thinking process into the solution of the problem posed by the task. The attainment of the final task is thus conceived to be a matter of successive attainment and "integration" of a series of lower level learning sets, beginning with those which are already available to the learner.
> (Gagné and Paradise, 1961, p.2)

The results tended to support Gagné's theory and the numbers of subjects who learned the higher elements without possessing the relevant subordinate ones were small but not zero, as they should have been if the hierarchy was correct (Gagné and Paradise, 1961). A similar result, but with fewer exceptions to the postulated hierarchy, was found in the next experimental investigation of mathematical subject matter (Gagné, Mayor, Garstens and Paradise, 1962).

Despite the importance of the implications of Gagné's early work, few investigations of the validity of hierarchies were performed in the subsequent decade (White, 1973). Those that did take place did not always confirm the existence of the postulated hierarchy. For example, Kolb (1967-8) found that many subjects passed tests of higher elements dealing with basic ideas of ratio and line-segment graphs, having failed at the lower ones. Although in later experiments subjects behaved in ways which did not fit the proposed hierarchies and consequently brought the theory into disrepute, White (1973) suggested that the studies were at fault because of their unsatisfactory design. Bergan (1980), however, disagreed with White and suggested that the results arose from the limitations in the learning hierarchy itself. One limitation is that Gagné's model does not include a set of equations describing the relationships among variables in the model. Such equations could be beneficial in estimating the magnitude of influence of variables in the model. The major limitation seems to be the restriction of the description of the relationships depicted in the model to two conditions: a skill is either prerequisite or it is not, no other possibilities are allowed. This fails to take account of the varieties of relationships that could exist.

> There could be reciprocal causal relationships between skills on the same level in a hierarchy. Unspecified variables outside the model could be exerting a significant influence on skill learning. There could be relationships among variables that have no simple causal interpretation. Finally, a skill placed in a hierarchy by virtue of one prerequisite relationship could influence several other skills at different levels in the hierarchy without being prerequisite to any of them. (Bergan, 1980, p.628)

There is nevertheless great appeal in the idea of learning hierarchies and it is an integral part of Bloom's approach to learning for mastery. Bloom (1976) does, however, acknowledge that not all learning tasks contain hierarchical arrangements of elements.

Learning For Mastery Strategies

Bloom (1968) acknowledged the fact that there were many different strategies for mastery learning, but that each strategy should deal effectively with the variables described by Carroll (1963).

He suggested that one ideal strategy would be to have a good tutor for each individual student, but acknowledged that this is not possible on a large scale on economic grounds. Nevertheless, the tutor-student relationship is a useful model to consider when working out the details of a more economically viable strategy.

Other strategies suggested include allowing students to go at their own pace, guiding students as to the most suitable courses, and providing different tracks or streams.

Bloom and his colleagues, following in Morrison's footsteps at the University of Chicago, experimented with various mastery strategies using diagnostic procedures and alternative methods and materials as supplements to regular classroom instruction. With such an approach the aim was to bring all students up to mastery standard within the regular term or period of calendar time in which the course was usually taught.

The strategy required specification of the 'preconditions' necessary, the development of 'operating procedures' and evaluation of the 'outcomes' of the strategy.

Pre-conditions

To develop mastery learning it is necessary, according to Bloom, to define what mastery is and whether or not a student has achieved it. Specification of objectives and content of instruction are, therefore, necessary preconditions. The translation of these into evaluation procedures is also necessary. Implicit in defining outcomes and evaluation procedures is the distinction between the teaching-learning process and the evaluation process. The teaching-learning is intended to prepare a student for achievement of a specific level of competence in an area of learning. The summative evaluation at the end of a course is intended to determine the extent to which this has been achieved. This is not a competitive approach to education because Bloom sees much of learning and development being destroyed by primary emphasis on competition.

The LFM approach relies on setting standards of mastery and excellence, followed by a strategy to bring as many students as possible to this standard. One method employed was to base the standards for the new approach on those achieved by the top group prior to the introduction of the mastery approach. In this way students were informed of the performance required but were not in competition for grades, they were to be judged on the basis of levels of mastery actually obtained by students in the previous year. This enabled a more co-operative approach, students helping each other without the fear that special advantage was being given.

Operating Procedures

Bloom's mastery approach was based on materials and methods used in previous years, within a similar timetable, in the belief that requiring extensive training of teachers would limit the acceptance of the new approach.

The operating procedures were used as supplements to the regular teaching. They were devised to ensure mastery of each learning unit in such a way as to reduce time required by altering quality of instruction and ability to understand the instruction. Two main operating procedures were adopted:

1. Formative and Summative Evaluation

The course was broken down into small units of learning, such as a chapter in a textbook, a time unit of the course or a well defined portion of a course, usually a week or two of learning activity.

Based on the ideas of Bloom (1956) and Gagné (1965) each unit was analysed into a number of elements ranging from specific terms or facts, to more complex abstract ideas such as concepts or principles and finally to applications of principles and the analysis of complex theoretical statements. Much of this initial work was conducted with such subjects as algebra and science topics, which fitted in well with Gagné's theoretical position on hierarchies of learning tasks.

Following from this breaking down of subject matter brief diagnostic progress tests were devised, which were then used to determine the extent of student mastery of a given unit. Such tests also indicated what the student still had to accomplish when he failed to reach the mastery criterion. These diagnostic tests were referred to as Formative Evaluation.

Frequent formative evaluation paces the students and helps motivate them, according to mastery theory, ensuring that each unit of learning is mastered before subsequent learning tasks are started. Early parts of the course may require more frequent formative testing than later sections, but there will be some variation in testing in various parts of a course.

Bloom believed that, for students who thoroughly mastered the unit, formative evaluation would reinforce the learning and reduce course anxiety about achievement.

Students lacking mastery of a particular unit had the specific deficits identified and particular instructional materials or processes were recommended to correct the learning. A very specific prescription was seen as being essential for students failing a formative test.

The test was not graded other than as showing mastery or non-mastery because Bloom believed that giving different point-grades (A, B, C, etc.) could be counter-productive.

Thus, the main purpose of the formative evaluation was to determine the degree of mastery of a given learning task and to identify those aspects of the task which were not mastered.

> The purpose is not to grade or certify the learner; it is to help both the learner and the teacher focus upon

the particular learning necessary for movement toward mastery. (Bloom, Hastings and Madaus, 1971, p.61)

The term 'summative evaluation' was given to the much more general assessment of the degree to which the 'larger outcomes have been attained over the entire course.' Such summative evaluation could be used to grade pupils and to report to parents or administrators. It was felt that several skills or concepts which combine to make a broader ability should be presented before a summative examination is administered. Summative tests should not be thought of only as end of course or final examinations, they could equally be used every four or six weeks to assess mid-term attainment of the various abilities taught in a course.

Bloom, Hastings and Madaus (1971) suggest that it is the level of generalization which differentiates summative from formative evaluation, and they indicate that summative assessment is linked to Tyler's more general descriptions of desired behaviours, whereas formative evaluation is more closely allied to Gagné's detailed prerequisite capabilities for each large aim.

2. Alternative Learning Resources

Bloom found that students do attempt to work on their difficulties if they are given specific suggestions of what to do. The best procedure identified was to have small groups of students (two or three) meet regularly for up to an hour each week to review the results of formative tests and to help each other overcome difficulties. Tutorial assistance was found not to be as popular as peer group meetings for secondary and higher education students. Other types of learning resource prescriptions, recommended by Bloom, were:

1. Rereading pages of the original instructional materials.
2. Reading alternative materials.
3. Use of specific pages of workbooks or programmed texts.
4. Use of selected a-v aids.

Ryan and Schmidt (1979) identified the most successful corrective strategies as being those which include objectives plus a problem testing the objectives of the previous lesson, discussion of the problem, specific prescriptions for using the text, class notes and handouts, and alternative resources, such as texts, workbooks, games and kits. When correctives consisted of objectives or problems only their effectiveness was considerably diminished.

Affective and Cognitive Consequences of LFM

Bloom suggested that if a system of formative and summative evaluation informs the student of his mastery of the subject, he will come to believe in his own mastery and competence and this will change his view of himself and the world.

He will certainly begin to respond more positively to the subject he has mastered. Mastery will provide the necessary reassurance and reinforcement to help the student to view himself as adequate thus contributing to positive mental health:

> Finally, modern society requires continual learning throughout life. If the schools do not promote adequate learning and reassurance of progress, the student must come to reject learning - both in the school and later in life. Mastery learning can give zest to school learning and can develop a life-long interest in learning. It is this continual learning which should be the major goal of the educational system. (Bloom, 1968/81, p.174)

Bloom's initial description of the cognitive outcomes described results for an experiment conducted from 1965 to 1967. Using the standards of grading adopted in 1965, prior to the introduction of a mastery approach, the aim was to use a variety of techniques during ensuing years to turn all students into 'A' students (ie. all students in the years 1966 and 1967 would obtain the same grades, using the same criteria, as were obtained by the top students of 1965). The results indicated that for 1967 80% of students obtained the level of mastery previously associated with 'A' grade students and by 1967 this had risen to 90% of students. The techniques certainly appeared to work in these initial studies and led to further investigations.

Learning For Mastery: The Research

Bloom (1976) summarized the early research on the mastery approach in 'Human Characteristics and School Learning.' These were 'a series of small experimental and school-based studies' in which students from the University of Chicago contrasted mastery with traditional methods.

Cognitive entry behaviours were measured at the beginning of each learning task, using a formative diagnostic test, and students were tested again at the end of the teaching session. Those students in the mastery groups received additional tuition, as indicated by the formative diagnostic test, if they failed to reach the set mastery criterion. They were then tested again after these 'corrective procedures' using a parallel form of formative test.

If Bloom's theory is correct we would expect a student's performance on one learning task to be highly correlated with performance on the next task, in the traditional group. The best students in this group would perform well on the first task and this would enable them to perform at an equally high level on the next task.

This would not be the case in the mastery group because those students who were failing to reach mastery on the initial task would receive appropriate materials and time to enable them to reach a position previously associated with the more able students. Having gained this position they would be just as likely to perform at a higher level in the next task. Thus, their performance on the original task would not be predictive of their performance on the second task. That at least is the theory, and it also predicts that there would be high correlations between one task score and the next task score for traditional courses, but much smaller (or even zero) correlations between one task and the next for mastery groups.

Bloom (1976) quotes studies covering subjects such as second language acquisition, matrix algebra, probability and an 'imaginary' science. The correlations between achievement on the first learning task in the series and the final (summative) achievement are:

	Mastery	Non-mastery
Anderson (1973)	0.31	0.68
Arlin (1973)	0.19	0.49
Block (1970)	0.44	0.78
Levin (1975)	0.59	0.72
Ozcelik (1974)	0.36	0.48
Median	0.36	0.68

These results demonstrate an overall agreement with Bloom's prediction from his theory, although the mastery correlations do not reach the zero figure that Bloom had hoped for. There is a definite trend for a much reduced correlation between initial performance and final performance under mastery conditions. The larger correlation of 0.68 for non-mastery students indicates the extent to which performance on the initial learning task will influence the final achievement when there are no correctives for defective learning.

Table 4-1. Mean performance scores for Mastery and Non-mastery groups.

	LEARNING TASK 1		LEARNING TASK 2		LEARNING TASK 3		
	Orig. Ach.	Corr. Ach.	Orig. Ach.	Corr. Ach.	Orig. Ach.	Corr. Ach.	Summ. Ach.
Mastery Groups	63	85	69	87	71	86	76
Non-mastery Groups	63		55		54		44

Orig. Ach. - Original achievement after instruction on learning task.
Corr. Ach. - Corrected achievement (mastery group only) after receiving additional corrective instruction.
Summ. Ach. - Summative achievement on completion of three tasks.

Of further interest is the average cumulative performance of the five experimental groups reported by Bloom (1976) given in Table 4.1. The non-mastery group does not receive correctives and, therefore, is represented by one score only for each of the three hierarchically arranged learning tasks. This is called the 'Original Achievement' score. The mastery group receives correctives after each learning task, for those failing to reach the criterion level, and takes a parallel form of the test giving a 'Corrected Achievement' score in addition to the 'Original Achievement' score. The difference between the 'Original Achievement' score and the 'Corrected Achievement' score represents the improvement in the mastery group following the correctives procedure. This improvement in performance for the mastery group results in a larger difference between the groups on the next learning task. With each set of correctives we see the gap between the mastery and non-mastery group increasing: initially, there is no difference; on the second task in the hierarchy there is a difference of 14%, in favour of the mastery group; and on the third task this has further increased to 17%. The final summative average difference is 32%, in favour of the mastery group.

These results were indicative of the scale of improvements possible with a mastery learning approach, and

Table 4-2. Student achievement in mastery and non-mastery conditions. (Based on Kim, 1971)

Instructional Treatment	Percentage of Students Achieving Mastery			
	English	Maths	Physics	Biology
Mastery	50	48	30	22
Non-Mastery	44	26	8	3

were confirmed by the research studies reviewed by Block (1974).

Block quotes the work of Kim (1971) and his colleagues (Lee et al., 1971) as showing the power of LFM. In these studies, using a group-based, mastery learning strategy, with pupil-teacher ratios of 70:1, Kim and his colleagues converted much of the Korean elementary and middle-school system into a mastery model. The pilot study taught 272 seventh grade students an eight-session unit on geometry. Kim found that 75% of the mastery group scored at the mastery criteria of 80% correct, compared with only 40% of the traditionally taught students reaching this level.

On the basis of this successful experiment Kim expanded his next study to 5,800 students, who studied maths and english over an eight week period. In English, 75% of mastery students reached the 80% criterion, compared with 28% of the traditional group; in maths, 67% of mastery students reached the criterion, against 39% of the traditional group.

The third experiment was much larger in scope. Rural and urban pupils learned maths, English, physics and biology over a full school year. There were 25,887 students in the experiment. The results were quite impressive (Table 4-2), with 2,000-3,000 more students gaining mastery in maths, physics and biology when compared with traditional methods.

Similar results were obtained by Lee et al. (1971), for arithmetic and science when taught to 12,504 pupils in 5th and 6th grades, with 27-32% more pupils reaching the 80% criterion under mastery conditions.

These differences in performance demonstrate the scale of achievement possible for students who are not reaching their maximum potential under normal instructional circumstances. Block (1974) applauds the magnitude of the successful application of mastery learning:

> Here a difference of a few percentage points, let alone differences of 20 to 30 points, between the percentage of students reaching a high performance level under mastery conditions and the percentage reaching the same level under nonmastery learning conditions translates into differences of thousands of students who are achieving levels in their learning they might never ordinarily have reached. (Block, 1974, p.34)

Further research on mastery learning in the classroom was summarized by Block and Burns (1977) in 'Review of Research in Education' (vol. 4), edited by L.S. Shulman. In this later paper the authors reported a meta-analysis on the research, giving an average effect size for the LFM-taught students of 0.83, which would move the average student in the non-mastery group from the 50th position in class to the top 20% of the class, a large educational effect. Keller studies were also included in this review and before discussing the overall results a description of Keller's 'Personalized System Of Instruction' is necessary.

KELLER'S PERSONALIZED SYSTEM OF INSTRUCTION

Keller describes the the first steps towards his system as having taken place during an evening brain-storming session involving Keller and three other psychologist colleagues, who had been invited to set up a new department of Psychology in the University of Brazilia, in 1963. They were given absolute freedom to follow their own dictates and fancies in carrying out the task.

Whereas Bloom had adapted the work of Carroll and Gagné, Keller's group was overtly 'operant' in its orientation, or as Keller put it 'tarred with the brush of reinforcement theory.' They were excited by Skinner's Natural Science Course at Harvard University, and all were convinced that traditional teaching methods were hopelessly out-of-date, and were impressed by the teaching machine and programmed-instruction movement.

They were not the only ones disillusioned with traditional methods of instruction. In the late 1950s and early 1960s educational researchers raised some unsettling questions about the effectiveness of most college teaching. In a number of major studies, investigators found that they could reduce by more than two-thirds the amount of time students spent in the classroom without affecting end-of-course student achievement (Kulik and Jaksa, 1977). Dubin & Taveggia (1968) went even further and demonstrated that such typical classroom activities as lectures and discussions might be eliminated completely without altering student achievement. Pooling data from 91 studies conducted between

1924 and 1965 they showed that students learned as much from independent study as they did from more conventional approaches to teaching. In fact, one of the chapters in Dubin and Taveggia's 'The Teaching-Learning Paradox' is titled "THERE ARE NO DIFFERENCES", in very large capital letters.

On the basis of these research results many innovators believed that students could learn as much through the newer approaches as they had learned from the more traditional approaches. And some even believed that they might actually improve learning.

According to the behaviouristic approach of Keller and his colleagues students are more likely to perform well if they find satisfaction in their studies or in behaviouristic terms 'The consequences of learning are important instructional contingencies.'

This means that positive consequences (instructor praise, good grades, feelings of achievement) are considered to be much more effective facilitators of learning than negative consequences (boredom, failure, or other forms of punishment).

External rewards are important, but it was thought that for adult learners they were not nearly as important as the general internal rewards (feelings of achievement, satisfaction or accomplishment).

Keller's 'Personalized System of Instruction' (PSI), which is also known as the 'Keller Plan', is based on these principles. It specifies objectives and provides reinforcement for their successful achievement, as well as giving the student more options and opportunities for personal interaction than traditional instructional systems.

The system was first publicly announced in 1968 in Keller's article 'Goodbye, teacher', which appeared in the new 'Journal of Applied Behaviour Analysis'. It begins with the chant:

> Goodbye scholars, goodbye school
> Goodbye teacher, darned old fool

and goes on to describe Keller's reasons for being disillusioned with the traditional classroom and formal education. He also outlines some of his observations made during his time in a military training centre. This is what he says about that centre:

> I should have seen many things that I didn't see at all, or saw very dimly. I could have noted, for example, that instruction in such a centre was highly individualised, in spite of large classes, sometimes permitting students to advance at their own speed throughout a course of study. I could have seen the clear specification of

> terminal skills for each course, together with the carefully graded steps leading to this end. I could have seen the demand for perfection at every level of training and for every student; the employment of classroom instructors who were little more than the successful graduates of earlier classes; the minimizing of the lecture as a teaching device and the maximizing of student participation. I could have seen, especially, an interesting division of labour in the educational process, wherein the non-commissioned, classroom teacher was restricted to duties of guiding, clarifying, demonstrating, testing, grading, and the like, while the commissioned teacher, the training officer, dealt with matters of course logistics, the interpretation of training manuals, the construction of lesson plans and guides, the evaluation of student progress, the selection of non-commissioned cadre, and the writing of reports for his superiors. (Keller, 1968, p.80)

Much of the Personalized System of Instruction can be seen as a development of Keller's observations of military training - perhaps one reason for the emphasis on instruction, rather than 'education' or 'teaching'. There are five main elements in PSI as described in the 1968 paper:

1. The unit-perfection requirement for advance, which lets the student go ahead to new material only after demonstrating mastery of the preceding unit.
2. The go-at-your-own pace feature, which permits a student to move through the course at a speed commensurate with his ability and other demands upon his time.
3. The stress upon the written word in teacher-student communications.
4. The use of proctors, which permits repeated testing, immediate scoring, almost unavoidable tutoring, and a marked enhancement of the personal-social aspect of the educational process.
5. The use of lectures and demonstrations as vehicles of motivation, rather than sources of critical information.

Mastery

Mastery learning proposes that all or almost all students can master what they are taught. It enables 90-95% of students to achieve the same high level as the top 25% learning under typical group-based instructional methods. Under such circumstances it is assumed that students will learn more material in less time and there will be greater student interest in and attitude toward the subject learned than is found in traditional classrooms.

Keller indicates that the mastery requirement means an essentially perfect performance. It is acceptable to interpret this as each student answering nine out of ten questions correctly, provided the single error is corrected. Any further compromise with mastery is unwise because:

> the requirement of eighty-five percent will automatically raise questions as to why eighty-three percent isn't 'close enough.' There will be requests for 'partial credit.' An adversary system with 'bargaining' about grades quickly returns to the classroom. The mutual respect and high morale upon which the course depends deteriorates. The course policy statement should specify that the criterion for a pass is perfection. (Keller and Sherman, 1974, p.37)

Self-pacing

One of the essential characteristics of mastery learning is the time spent in study and this leads to the emphasis, in the Keller Plan, placed on a completely student-paced programme of study.

It is important to stress that the system places no restraints on the student's study time - thus a student may elect to take a unit quiz at her convenience or when she is most ready to demonstrate mastery, rather than at a time for all students which is dictated by the instructor.

The self-pacing allows for individual differences in rate of study and is essential if the level of achievement is held constant. This is because in essence it is not possible to hold both level of individual achievement and rate of completion constant. Traditional lecture methods, for example, hold rate of completion constant and, because of this, level of achievement varies widely. However, in PSI courses tests can be taken at any time and can be repeated as required, and the result is that while the average student evidences a steady progress, at any one time individual students will be working on different units and taking different tests. Here we have mastery level of achievement held constant and so the rate of completion varies.

Written Materials

Keller in 'Goodbye, Teacher' summarizes his use of written materials by stating that PSI places stress upon the written word in teacher-student communication. Although programmed texts are used, Keller emphasizes that the steps in a PSI programme are not frames in a set; they are more inclusive and can be better described as reading assignments or laboratory exercises. Also, he states in a later description of PSI that television, computers and teaching machines may all be used in the system but should not be equated with the system.

PSI courses are based upon a standard textbook, journal articles, other readings and are supplemented by a study guide. This guide breaks the course into units. Each guide consists of an introduction, statement of objectives, procedure, study questions, and supplementary materials as dictated by the specific course.

The study guide is designed to allow the student to work through the material independently and this function over-rides the form the guide might take. A typical guide has four sections:

1. Introduction: in which the instructor comments upon the textbook and supplements it. It may point out differing views to those expressed in the text and correct deficiencies.
2. Statement of objectives: which indicates the goals of the study unit in behavioural terms. It tells the student what he will be able to do on completion of the unit. The objectives should be very specific, but make the work interesting at the same time.
3. Study questions: these should help the student to detect his progress and success, and may include concepts or technical terms that require defining and problems for completion.
4. Procedure: this section specifies the activities necessary for completion of the unit objectives. It may consist only of the assignment to be read, or it may be more detailed, providing an indication of specific pages to be read and the order for working through different articles. A page-and-line key of special instructions may be included where the textbook is found to be inadequate.

Keller and Sherman (1974) indicate that a well-written procedure section tells the students what to do, how to self-test comprehension, how to decide whether to proceed or review and how to decide when they have finished.

The study guide may include any further information that helps the students to complete their work successfully, the main criterion for a study guide being that it works.

Student Proctors

These are usually students who have successfully completed the course. Their job is to score quizzes, discuss answers, tutor students who are experiencing difficulties, and provide feedback to the instructor on the course in general.

According to Keller, the proctor is a vital component of the system, being a primary source of external reward for the mastery of each unit; they constitute the personal contact between student and system and provide immediate feedback to the students. The proctor allows interaction between the student and the system and a degree of flexibility that can only come from human interaction: credit can be given to a student if he appears to understand the item tested, even though the answer to the item was incorrect due to some minor error. Also the proctor can discuss correct responses in order to determine whether the answer is guessed or arrived at for invalid reasons. This is what Keller says of the 'proctor':

> The proctor is the new link in the chain. His principal job is that of decreasing the gap of understanding between the student and teacher - a gap that is sometimes very wide.
> He can do this because he has a repertoire of behaviour that is intermediate between the two with respect to the subject matter of the course. He may find logic in an answer that an instructor would never have perceived; he may restate a question in a way that brings out evidence of knowledge; and he may by example or parallel statement strengthen a student's grasp of a concept. He provides the individual consideration that a student may never have had before.
> (Keller and Sherman, 1974, p.20-1)

The proctor is helped in his work by 4 factors:

1. his experience with a similar course in which he was recently successful;
2. a weekly proctor's meeting in which every question on every test may be discussed;
3. a handy list of acceptable answers to the questions, to jog his memory if needed;
4. usually, relevant knowledge from advanced courses within the same subject-matter field.

Those proctors, described above, are called by Keller 'grading proctors', and he estimates that ten or more would be required for a class of one hundred students. Two further proctors may be involved in the general scheme: (1) the testing proctor; and (2) the study hall proctor.

1. Testing proctor: is responsible for all record-keeping and actually administering the tests. Keller says that this non-educational role may be undertaken by a reliable clerk or by grading proctors on a rotational basis.

2. Study hall proctor: this position is so important that it may be filled by the instructor or his assistant. He stands between the textbook and the student (just as the grading proctor stands between student and the instructor). He clarifies obscure passages, helps with difficult operations, explains unintelligible references etc. The study hall proctor generally serves a small percentage of the class (usually its weakest members) and the number of cries for help will decrease as study habits are improved and students gain in self-reliance.

Keller says that the study-hall proctor may be selected on the basis of course history, achievement or special aptitudes but also cautions that if he acts too much like a teacher he may not be the most effective promoter of learning in the classroom.

In addition to the proctors there is the classroom assistant whose tasks include distribution of assignments, study questions, checking of supplies, maintenance of progress charts etc. Later, he may take the place of the instructor at various meetings and in general give the instructor time to alter the course as and when necessary.

The instructor's role is that of a manager of learning. He selects and analyses the material to be mastered, he decides how to present it, and constructs the various questions based upon it. Keller emphasizes that the textbooks must be carefully read before selection to determine their suitability for students who will be questioned upon it in detail - errors, confusions and contradictions that might go unnoticed in a conventional system will stand out as 'unsightly blemishes' in PSI.

The instructor is also responsible for dividing material into suitable units, devising suitable study questions to help students and test questions for the mastery test. He will receive a great deal of information on everything he has devised for the course and as a result he will be responsible for the continual modification of the system, as he aims for perfection.

Lectures

Lectures are used for enrichment rather than to transmit information, which in PSI is done through the use of study guides and the text. Lectures are given to demonstrate the excitement of the discipline; and may be used to show films or for other special events such as visiting speakers. They serve a purely supplemental function. As Keller and Sherman point out:

> A few lectures are useful. The instructor can serve as a model, impart style, even provide inspiration. In fact we may expect a very polished and challenging presentation now that such events are infrequent. Such lectures must be fine indeed; otherwise they will not attract an audience. Since the lecture is given for motivational reasons rather than for the transmittal of essential information, PSI lectures are 'extras' and not required. (Keller and Sherman, 1954, pp.41-42)

Personalized System of Instruction: The Research

In the 'Review of Research in Education' (1975) McKeachie & Kulik summarized the results of the available evaluations of PSI:

1. Keller plan is an attractive teaching method to most students. In published reports students rate Keller plan more favourably than teaching by lecture.
2. Self-pacing and interaction with tutors seem to be features most favoured by students. There are reports of higher-than-average student drop-out rates for Keller courses.
3. Content learning, as measured by final examinations, is adequate: in published studies final examination performance always equals and usually exceeds performance in lecture sections.
4. Students almost invariably report that they learn more from PSI and report expending more time and effort.

In addition to these generally favourable reports evidence was also accumulating which showed the relative importance of the various components of PSI in contributing to the system's overall successful performance.

Student Ratings of the Course

Gallup (1970) found favourable comments on a psychology

PSI course from 98% of students and Born & Herbert (1971) found that only 7 of 145 students would not recommend the course to other students. When looking at Library Science, Knightly & Sayre (1972) found that the self-paced mode of instruction was considered better than lecture courses by 100% of students; the course being rated as 'above average' or 'one of the best' by 93%.

Perhaps it should be noted here that in the early days many academics tended to describe PSI as a de-humanizing, programmed approach to instruction, and stress its links with Skinner's behaviourist orientation. Students who studied such courses, however, liked its freedom, self-determination and personal interaction!

Features Rated Highly by Students

Green (1971) categorized student comments about Keller courses and reported that the feature most often praised is the freedom of pace. In another study, Nelson & Scott (1972) had students rank 12 features of PSI. Most important were (1) self-pacing; (2) interactions with teaching assistant or instructor; (3) small unit steps; (4) discussions with proctors. Self-pacing was also seen to be the feature rated most highly in a similar study by Myers (1970). Clearly, for the students, the most attractive features of PSI are self-pacing and personalized interactions.

Green (1971) reported that 90% of students on Keller plan took further Keller options when offered; and Gallup (1974) reported that he had to limit student numbers on his course when it was introduced as a Keller type option.

This overall positive response to PSI was not consonant with McKeachie & Kulik's (1975) suggestion that student drop-out was higher than the average for conventional lecture courses. For example, Keller presented data that showed withdrawal rates of about 20% - no comparison data was available, but 20% does seem to be very high. Sheppard & MacDermot (1970) reported a drop-out rate of 17% for a Keller course on introductory course, compared with 6% for a traditional class. Born (1971) also presented data showing a withdrawal rate of 14%, 25% and 14% for Keller sections compared with 5%, 6% and 5% for conventional courses.

However, it is not the whole story. McMichael & Corey's (1969) results showed a high drop-out rate for the PSI course, but a slightly higher one for the conventional lecture course: 12% compared with 13%. Kulik, Kulik and Cohen (1979) in their meta-analysis of PSI research found that of 27 investigations which reported comparisons of course completion, the differences between PSI and conventional courses were trivial.

Procrastination did seem to be a major disadvantage of

such a self-paced system of instruction in the early days and Green (1971) and others suggested ways in which it could be prevented:

1. publishing a recommended schedule of dates for passing units, which will yield a steady rate of work,
2. making admittance to 'fun' lectures contingent upon passing units,
3. offering early final exams for students finishing the course early.

Content Learning

Kulik, Kulik and Smith (1976) presented details of 39 studies which satisfied their basic requirements of sound experimental design. In 38 of the 39 studies final exam performance was better in the PSI course. In 34 of the comparisons the difference was considered to be statistically reliable. The authors state that the differences were large enough to have practical significance: they show that for a typical result a student, who is average on a standard test, scoring 50% in a typical lectures-based course, would score 75% if she takes the PSI courses, indicating an Effect Size of 0.66. A later meta-analysis (Kulik, Kulik, and Cohen, 1979) found 61 studies which compared PSI and conventional teaching. PSI final examinations were 8 percentage points higher, giving an average effect size of 0.49. Also, there was 35% less variation in the scores for the PSI group. These results refer to final examinations. But what about the long-term impact PSI has on students? Again, Kulik, Kulik and Cohen (1979) indicated that PSI comes out with better results. In fact the differences were greater after the retention period (which varied from 3 weeks to 15 months), suggesting that final exams, if anything, underestimate the magnitude of PSI's effect.

Another way in which the effects of PSI can be investigated is the transfer study, where students study, for example, MATHS 1 by either PSI or conventional methods. They then study MATHS 2 together in a conventional class. How does PSI affect performance in MATHS 2 ? The transfer studies all indicate that those students who take the PSI option for the initial course out-perform conventionally taught students on the second course, even though the second course is a conventionally taught course.

Component Analysis

There can be no doubt that PSI is effective, the question is, why is PSI so effective? Various studies have attempted to throw some light on this question, and have looked at the various components of PSI.

The research studies tend to show that small units are important to the effectiveness of PSI - if the units become too long PSI's effectiveness deteriorates (Calhoun, 1976). Semb (1974) also found better performance in major exams for students working on smaller units. Nelson and Bennett (1973) and O'Neill et al (1975) found more consistent progress in shorter unit PSI courses.

Feedback also seems to be important and there are several studies in which groups receiving delayed feedback were compared with groups receiving immediate feedback (Calhoun, 1976; Farmer et al, 1972; and Johnson and Sulzer-Azaroff, 1974). The achievement of the delayed feedback groups was significantly lower than groups receiving immediate feedback.

Relaxation of the mastery criterion leads to a decline in the effectiveness of PSI, as was anticipated by Keller. Semb in 1974 showed that a high mastery criterion (100%) produced better final test performance than a low mastery criterion (60%) and this was confirmed in a later study (Phillips and Semb, 1975).

Surprisingly, the proctors don't seem to be an essential feature of PSI. Blackburn, Semb and Hopkins (1975) compared a Keller PSI course with a section which included self-grading (the proctors only acting as administrators). In the final exam both groups performed equally well. Calhoun (1976) compared written feedback with feedback provided by the proctor and again there were differences, but they were not statistically significant.

Research studies have also failed to show that self-pacing is important. Several studies show no difference on final examination or student evaluation for teacher-paced and self-paced groups (Beneke and Taylor, 1975; Calhoun, 1976; Lewis, 1972).

Although Keller recommends lectures in PSI courses as motivational agents, some instructors have built in conventional lectures in addition to the individualised work. Calhoun (1976) found that twice-weekly lectures did not improve the performance of PSI students and Minke and Carlson (1973) found that adding lectures did not change the percentage of students passing, the withdrawal rate or the overall evaluation of students passing the course.

LFM AND PSI: A REVIEW OF THE RESEARCH

The research on mastery learning as found in the approaches of Bloom and Keller was summarized in a comprehensive review by Block and Burns (1977). In this paper the authors reported a meta-analysis on the research, giving the effect size for LFM achievement comparisons and a combined retention effect size for PSI and LFM.

A total of 97 comparisons were identified, involving different types and numbers of students. Mastery students scored higher than non-mastery students 89% of the time, and statistically significantly higher 61% of the time. For retention (combining PSI and LFM) the mastery students were almost always superior to the non-mastery groups, significantly so 63% of the time. The average effect size for the LFM-taught students was 0.83. A similar large effect size was obtained from studies of LFM and PSI which included a retention test, with an average retention effect size of 0.67.

In addition, Block and Burns looked at the variability in learning. According to Bloom's theory the mastery approach will lead to greater uniformity in learning when compared to traditional methods, which should show increasing variability. In 80 studies comparing variance in achievement test scores, mastery students showed less variation in their scores 74% of the time, and less variability in retention scores 85% of the time. The reduction in variance was approximately 50% for both achievement and retention measures.

Kinds of Learning

Block and Burns also looked at learning in qualitative terms. They found some evidence to suggest that mastery strategies may be more likely to elicit higher order than lower order behaviours. Several researches found that mastery students were superior on essay-type questions that included comprehension, application, analysis, synthesis and evaluation skills, and that mastery students were more able to deal with these complex high order skills than the lower order multiple-choice knowledge questions.

There was some evidence, however, that for retention periods of 6 or 18 months it was the lower order behaviours associated with knowledge, rather than the complex application or analysis-synthesis, that were retained at a higher level in the mastery group.

The mastery approaches typically elicited more favourable affective responses from students, in particular there was a positive impact on students' interest in and attitudes to the subject matter, and also on self-concept, academic self-confidence, attitudes to co-operative learning and towards instruction. Although there is some evidence to suggest that mastery set at the 100% level adversely affects such attitudes and that an optimum figure of 90% maintains both the positive affective and achievement responses.

Time Consequences

A group of studies investigated the amount of time spent in learning in mastery and non-mastery groups. Uniformly, they found that mastery strategies had a homogenizing effect on differences in study time. One study found that differences were reduced from 7 to 1, to 4 to 1 by mastery methods, and that there was progressively less variability in the mastery study time. In the final unit of eight there was 90% less variability

Block and Burns comment that this reduction in individual differences in study time is purchased at the price of additional study time for the slower students. Over the short term there is an increase in the average study time required for mastery of 70-80%, compared with non-mastery. In the long term this may be reduced to 20-50%

The extra time is available from two sources. The first is the teacher who is encouraged to prepare and organize the instructional plans, procedures and materials outside of class time and prior to the instruction. This allows more time for interaction with the students. The student can also be encouraged to exert more effort, especially in overcoming procrastination, and various incentive schemes have been used, such as frequent testing, varying the size of learning units, teacher/peer pacing of instruction. The emphasis is clearly on techniques that encourage teachers and students to spend more time learning as opposed to non-learning activities.

Achievements of the Behavioural Systems

In many ways the work of Bloom and Keller in their mastery learning systems represents the summit of achievement for the neo-behaviourist 'systems' approach to instruction. Both were built on firm, though differing, psychological principles and of all the applications of the behavioural science approach to the technology of education, LFM and PSI represent the only methods which consistently produce significant educational results. Clark (1983) attributes this to the emphasis placed on method, defined by Glaser (1976) as 'the conditions which can be implemented to foster acquisition of competence,' rather than on the media involved in the delivery of instruction, as represented by the physical science approach.

It is fitting that Benjamin S. Bloom, whose work has been central to the development of instructional science for a generation, should have the last words:

> If you can be moved to try these ideas with a few teachers in your school for even as short a period as three months, you can determine the validity and limits of these ideas where they belong - in your classrooms and with your teachers and students.

He continues:

> However, neither further opportunity for education nor increased financial support for education will do much to improve the education of each of our students. The answer does not lie in additional funds, new fads, or major and sweeping changes in the organization of our educational system. As I see it, the solution lies in our views about students and their learning. These have grown out of our practices and they will not be changed until we alter these practices. When the changed practices succeed in promoting more effective learning, both teachers and students will change their views. (Bloom, 1978, p.563)

REFERENCES

Beneke, W.M. and Taylor, D.C. (1975) Effects of Unit Deadlines on Performances in a PSI Course. Paper presented at the annual meeting of the American Psychological Association, Chicago.

Bergan, J.R. (1980) 'The structural analysis of behaviour: an alternative to the learning-hierarchy model', Review of Educational Research, 50, 4, 625-646.

Blackburn, T., Semb, G. and Hopkins, B.L. (1975) 'The comparative effects of self-grading versus proctor grading on class efficiency and student performance'. In J.M. Johnson (Ed) Behaviour Research and Technology in Higher Education. Springfield Ill.: Charles C. Thomas.

Block, J.H. (1971) Mastery Learning. London: Holt Rinehart & Winston: .

Block, J.H. (1974) Schools, Society and Mastery Learning. London: Holt, Rinehart and Winston.

Block, J.H. and Burns, R.B. (1977) 'Mastery learning'. In L.S. Shulman (Ed) Review of Research in Education. Volume 4. Itasca, Ill.: F.E. Peacock, 3-49.

Bloom, B.S. (1964) Stability and Change in Human Characteristics . New York: John Wiley.

Bloom, B.S. (1968/81) 'Learning For Mastery', (UCLA-CSEIP) The Evaluation Comment, 1(2). In B.S. Bloom (Ed) All Our Children Learning. London: McGraw-Hill.
Bloom, B.S. (1976) Human Characteristics and School Learning. New York: McGraw-Hill.
Bloom, B.S. (1978) 'New views of the learner - implications for instruction and curriculum', Educational Leadership, 35, 562-76.
Bloom, B.S. et al. (1956) Taxonomy of Educational Objectives Handbook I: Cognitive Domain. New York: McKay.
Bloom, B.S., Hastings, J.T. and Madaus, G.F. (1971) Handbook on Formative and Summative Evaluation. London: McGraw-Hill.
Born, D.G. (1971) Student Withdrawals in Personalized Instruction Courses. Paper presented at the meeting of the Rocky Mountain Psychological Association, Denver, May.
Born, D.G. and Herbert, E. (1971) 'A further study of personalized instruction in large university classes', Journal of Experimental Education, 40, 6-11.
Bruner, J.S. (1966) Toward a Theory of Instruction. Cambridge, Mass.: Harvard University Press.
Calhoun, J.F. (1976) 'The combination of elements in the personalized system of instruction', Teaching of Psychology, 3, 73-76.
Carroll, J. (1963) 'A model of school learning', Teachers College Record, 64, 723-733 .
Clark, R.E. (1983) 'Reconsidering the research on learning from media', Review of Educational Research, 53, 4, 445-459.
Dubin, R. and Taveggia, T.C. (1968) The Teaching Learning Paradox. University of Oregon Press: Eugene
Farmer, J., Lachter, G.D., Blaustein, J.L. and Brett, K. (1972) 'The role of proctoring in personalized instruction', Journal of Applied Behaviour Analysis, 5, 401-404.
Gagné, R.M. (1962a) 'The acquisition of knowledge', Psychological Review, 69(4), 355-365.
Gagné, R.M. (1965) The Conditions of Learning. (1st Edition) London: Holt, Rinehart and Winston.
Gagné, R.M., Mayor, J.R., Garstens, H.L. and Paradise, N.E. (1962) 'Factors in acquiring knowledge of a mathematical task', Psychological Monographs, 76(7), No.526.
Gagné, R.M. and Paradise, N.E. (1961) 'Abilities and learning sets in knowledge acquisition', Psychological Monographs, 75(14), Whole No. 518.
Gallup, H.F. (1970) Individual Instruction in an Introductory Psychology Course. Paper presented at the meeting of the American Psychological Association, Washington, D.C. (Sept.)
Gallup, H.F. (1974) Problems in the Implementation of a course in Personalized Instruction. In J.G. Sherman (Ed) PSI: 41 Germinal Papers. Menlo Pk., Cal.:Benjamin.

Glaser, R. (1976) 'Components of a psychology of instruction: towards a science of design', Review of Educational Research, 46(1), 1-24.

Green, B.A. (1971) 'Physics teaching by Keller Plan at MIT', American Journal of Physics, 39, 764-775.

Johnson, K.R. and Sulzer-Azaroff, B. (1974) The Effects of Different Proctoring Systems on Student Examination Performance and Preference. Paper presented at Second National Conference on Research and Technology in College and University Teaching. Georgia State University, Atlanta, GA. (Nov.)

Keller, F.S. (1968) 'Goodbye, Teacher', Journal of Applied Behaviour Analysis', 1, 79-87.

Keller, F.S. and Sherman, J.G. (1974) The Keller Plan Handbook. Menlo Park-California: Wa. Benjamin.

Kim, H. (1971) 'Mastery learning in the Korean middle schools', UNESCO Regional Office for Education in Asia, 6(1).

Knightly, J.J. and Sayre, J.L. (1972) 'Self-paced instruction for library science students', Journal of Education for Librarianship, 12, 193-197.

Kolb, J.R. (1967-68) 'Effects of relating mathematics to science instruction on the acquisition of quantitative science behaviours', Journal of Research in Science Teaching, 5, 174-182.

Kulik, J.A. and Jaksa, P. (1977) 'PSI and other educational technologies in college teaching', Educational Technology, 17, Sept. 12-19.

Kulik, J.A., Kulik, C.C. and Cohen, P.A. (1979) 'A meta-analysis of outcome studies of Keller's personalized system of instruction. American Psychologist, 34(4), 307-318.

Kulik, J.A., Kulik, C.C. and Smith, B. (1976) 'Research on the personalized system of instruction', Programmed Learning and Educational Technology, 13, 21-30.

Lee, Y.D. et al. (1971) Interaction Improvement Studies on the Mastery Learning Project - Final Report on Mastery Learning Programme. Educational Research Centre, Seoul National University. (Nov.)

Lewis, J.D. (1972) Manipulation of Two Variables in a Contingency-managed Statistics Class. Paper presented at the West Coast PSI Conference. California State University.

McKeachie, W.J. and Kulik, J.A. (1975) Effective college teaching. In F.N. Kerlinger (Ed) Review of Research in Education Vol.3 Itasca,Illinois: F.E. Peacock

McMichael, J. and Corey, J.R. (1969) 'Contingency management in an introductory psychology course produces better learning', Journal of Applied Behaviour Analysis, 2, 79-83.

Minke, K.A. and Carlson, J.G. (1973) A Comparison of Two Lecture Systems in Unit Mastery Instruction. Paper presented at the annual meeting of the American Psychological Association, Montreal. (Aug.)

Morrison, H.C. (1926) The Practice of Teaching in a Secondary School. University of Chicago Press: Chicago.

Myers, W.A. (1970) 'Operant learning principles applied to teaching introductory statistics', Journal of Applied Behaviour Analysis, 3, 213-220.

Nelson, T.F. and Bennet, M. (1973) 'Unit size and progress rates in self-paced instruction', Journal of College Science Teaching, 3(2).

Nelson, T.F. and Scott, D.W. (1972) 'Personalized instruction in educational psychology', Michigan Academician, 4, 293-302.

O'Neill, G.W., Johnston, J.M., Walters, W.M. and Rasheed, J.A. (1975) The Effects of Quantity of Assigned Material On College Student Academic Performance and Study Behaviour. In J.M. Johnston (Ed) Behaviour Research and Technology in Higher Education. Springfield, Illinois: Charles C. Thomas.

Phillips, T.W. and Semb, G. (1975) A Comparison of Pre-quiz and Post-quiz Lectures in a Contingency-managed University Course. Paper presented at the annual meeting of the American Association, Chicago. (Sept.)

Rowntree, D. (1977) Assessing Students: How Shall We Know Them? London: Harper and Row.

Ryan, D.W. and Schmidt, M. (1979) Mastery Learning: Theory, Research, and Implementation. Toronto, Ontario: The Ontario Institute for Studies in Education.

Semb, G. (1974) 'Personalized instruction: the effects of mastery criteria and assignment length on college student test performance', Journal of Applied Behaviour Analysis, 7, 61-69.

Sheppard, W.C. and MacDermot, H.G. (1970) 'Design and evaluation of a programmed course in introductory psychology', Journal of Applied Behavioural Analysis, 3, 5-11,

Skinner, B.F. (1954) 'The science of learning and the art of teaching', Harvard Educational Review, 24(2), 86-97.

Tyler, R.W. (1932) 'The construction of examinations in botany and zoology', Service Studies in Higher Education, Ohio State University, Bureau of Educational Research Monographs, 15, 49-50.

Washburne, C.W. (1922) 'Educational measurements as a key to individualizing instruction and promotions', Journal of Educational Research, 5, 195-206.

White, R.T. (1973) 'Research into learning hierarchies', Review of Educational Research, 43(3), 361-375.

CHAPTER 5

HUMAN INFORMATION PROCESSING AND THE AUDIO-VISUAL APPROACH TO EDUCATIONAL TECHNOLOGY

We receive information from a vast array of sources, some experienced directly and physically as we come into contact with our immediate environment, others experienced vicariously through media such as films and television, or through symbolic modes such as words or figures. Some of these are perceived through all our senses, while others are perceived through a more limited number of senses. Treichler (1967) presents a number of interesting conclusions, which may accord with many commonly held beliefs concerning the relationship between our senses and how we learn and remember (Figure 5-1), although they should be treated with caution because he gives no indication of their basis.

Figure 5-1. The Relative Effectiveness of the Primary Senses

WE LEARN:

1.0% THROUGH TASTE
1.5% THROUGH TOUCH
3.5% THROUGH SMELL
11.0% THROUGH HEARING
83.0% THROUGH SIGHT

PEOPLE GENERALLY REMEMBER:

10% OF WHAT THEY READ
20% OF WHAT THEY HEAR
30% OF WHAT THEY SEE
50% OF WHAT THEY SEE AND HEAR
70% OF WHAT THEY SAY AS THEY TALK
90% OF WHAT THEY SAY AS THEY DO A THING!

Treichler's views have been reinforced by the theoretical orientations of a number of influential writers concerned with the audio-visual movement. For example, Dale (1954) listed the following proven contributions of such materials:

1. They supply a concrete basis for conceptual thinking

and hence reduce meaningless word-responses of students.
2. They have a high degree of interest for students.
3. They make learning more permanent.
4. They offer a reality of experience which stimulates self-activity on the part of pupils.
5. They develop a continuity of thought; this is especially true of motion pictures.
6. They contribute to growth of meaning and hence to vocabulary development.
7. They provide experiences not easily obtained through other materials and contribute to the efficiency, depth, and variety of learning.

Figure 5-2. Dale's 'Cone of Experience'

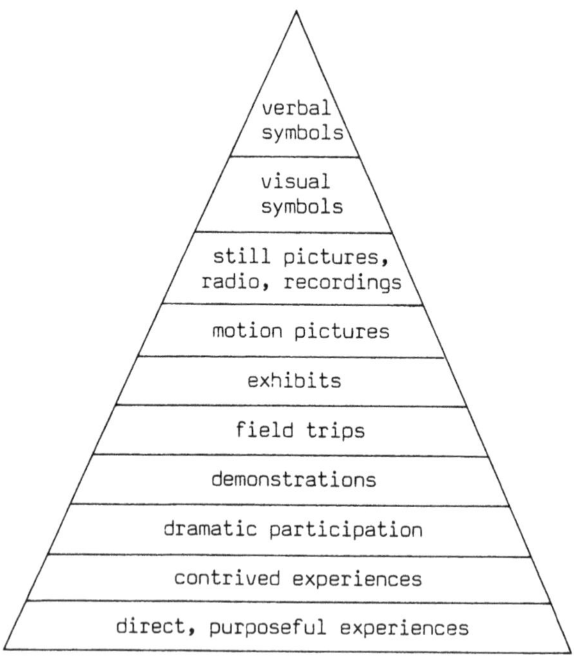

He concluded by asserting that these points do not constitute private beliefs or opinions, but are the 'distillation of a vast amount of research by many investigators.' Dale's 'Cone of Experience' (Figure 5-2) illustrates the narrowing of sensory experience from the concrete, purposeful experiences of direct, contingent experience to the higher reaches of abstract verbal and visual symbols. It reflects his original theoretical position that the predominant modes of instruction, found towards the pinnacle of the cone, provide restricted experiences for the pupil, who would greatly benefit from a more comprehensive range of educational experiences, encompassing those modes towards the base of the cone.

Early support for Dale's approach came from Carpenter (1953) in the form of the 'sign similarity hypothesis' which stated that:

> ...films whose signals, signs, and symbols have high degrees of similarity ('iconicity') to the objects and situation which they represent will be more effective for most instructional purposes than films whose signals, signs, and symbols have low degrees of 'iconicity'. (Carpenter, 1953, p. 41)

The term 'iconicity' was borrowed from Morris (1946), who suggested that signs vary in 'iconicity' to the degree to which they are similar to things or situations which they represent or signify. For example, a motion picture of a specific event may be described as highly iconic, whereas a pencil sketch may be described as being of low iconicity.

Such theories and other similar orientations (Knowlton, 1966; Gibson, 1954) have been given the collective term 'realism' theories by Dwyer (1978). In essence they suggest that the additional information flowing through several different sensory channels (ie. haptic, visual, auditory, etc.) will provide a multiplicity of stimuli which in turn will assist learners in organizing and structuring their perceptions, thereby ensuring more complete learning.

This approach has been preoccupied with the effects of the new media which were seen as being implicitly good because they were innovative devices that could supplant the verbal functions traditionally fulfilled by the teacher and text. Jonassen (1985) suggests that this materialistic conception of learning dominated the field in the early part of the century, yielding to the emergence of behaviourism towards the middle part of the century. In fact, it did not entirely give way and remained a powerful influence for several decades. Indeed, recent researches from cognitive psychology suggest that some, though by no means all, of the early claims may still be valid.

The major challenge to this physical science approach

to educational technology came from the emerging cognitive psychology of the 1950's and 1960's. This was epitomized by Travers (1964) who felt that the work of psychologists and researchers was at variance with the claims made by the proponents of the audio-visual movement. Travers concluded that:

> ...there does not seem to be a single contemporary scientist who takes the position that the human can receive more information if exposed to information transmitted through two sense modalities rather than one. The position of the research scientists and the designers of audio-visual materials are at such opposite poles that it hardly seems possible that both can be correct. (Travers, 1964, p.375)

Travers supported the idea that the human information processing system is best represented as a single channel of limited capacity and that increasing the available information to the human receiver, either by using several sensory modalities or using very realistic displays, will merely produce information overload, which in extreme cases will actually cause decreases in learning. His theoretical base was rooted in the work of many psychologists interested in the problems associated with human perception and communication, most notably that of Broadbent (1958).

This issue is a complex one. It has profound implications for education. On the one hand there are those who hold to the belief that direct, contingent experience, with multi-sensory inputs, is essential for intellectual development; and, set against these beliefs, are those which suggest that only a fraction of the total sensory information available at a given time is capable of being processed by the central nervous system and, therefore, that educators should aim to compress reality into a form most compatible with the central processing systems.

PSYCHOLOGICAL APPLICATIONS OF INFORMATION THEORY

Information theory was developed initially for communication systems such as the telephone or radio, the best known of the early models being that of Shannon and Weaver (1949), shown in Figure 5-3. According to Attneave (1959):

> The idea that information is measurable in precise terms was not widely appreciated until 1948, when Norbert Weiner's book "Cybernetics" appeared and Claude Shannon published a pair of articles titled "The Mathematical Theory of Communication"....The quick spread of

> Shannon's ideas beyond the field of engineering may be attributed largely to a skillful and imaginative introductory article by Warren Weaver which appeared in the July 1949 issue of Scientific American.
> (Forward to "Applications of Information Theory to Psychology").

In this system the message from the information source is converted into a signal by the transmitter, for example, a sentence spoken into a microphone which is broadcast by a radio transmitter. At some point this signal is contaminated by 'noise' (an electrical engineering term, denoting some form of interference), before being decoded by the receiver, eg. a radio receiver, and reconstituted as the message. As more 'noise' enters the system, so the intelligibility and

Figure 5-3. Shannon and Weaver's Linear Model of Communication (Shannon and Weaver, 1949)

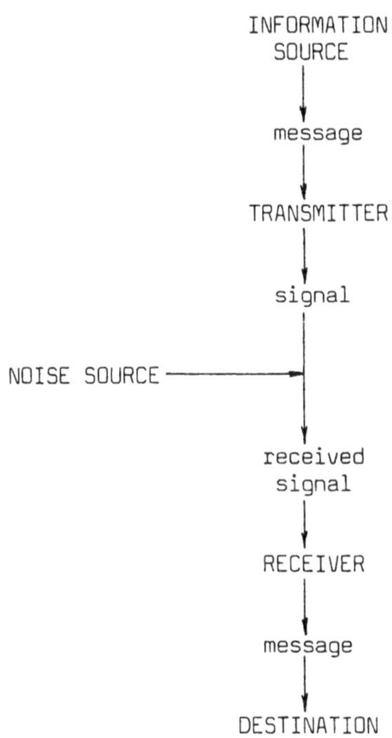

integrity of the original message changes, leading to new signals and information.

Shannon and Weaver viewed communication in a very broad sense to include all the procedures by which one mind may affect another: written and oral speech; music; pictorial arts; theatre; ballet; indeed, all human behaviour. Shannon's mathematical theory applied in the first instance only to the technical problem of accuracy of transference of various types of signals from sender to receiver. However, Weaver claimed that the theory was 'exceedingly general in its scope, fundamental in the problems it treats, and of classic simplicity and power in the results it reaches.'

The technical meaning of information is not radically different from every day usage, it is essentially 'choice', the narrowing down of alternatives, and the unit most often used for measurement is the 'bit', or binary digit. The word 'information' in communication theory relates not so much to what you do say, as to what you could say. The amount of information is defined in such a way that the nature of the information is irrelevant, just as weight is defined in such a way that the nature of the object is irrelevant: and the definition uses binary choice as its basis. In effect, the definition states that the information contained in a given situation, where a number of equally likely events could take place, is equal to the number of binary choices required to identify a specific event.

For example, imagine two boxes side by side, one of which contains an object (any object), with each box as likely to contain the object as the other. This situation represents one bit of information because it requires one binary choice to identify the box containing the object. No matter which box you choose to open you will know where the object is, and all uncertainty is removed. If you open the box and it is empty, you know unequivocally where the object is - in the other box! Of course, you also know where it is if you make the other choice. The point is, you only have to choose once to remove all uncertainty.

Thus, information is essentially choice, the narrowing down of alternatives. The mathematical theory of communication was developed in order to deal quantitatively with the transmission of messages over 'channels', to measure the amount of information transmitted, but Weaver indicated that the theory should not be restricted to engineering situations. It was to be seen as general in its scope.

The theory opened up a whole new avenue in psychology and some of Shannon's general concepts were rapidly introduced into the psychological literature by Miller and Frick in 1949. This led to a mushrooming of interest in information theory and its implications for the study of perception and communication. It was realized that, once received by the sensory apparatus, signals are then passed through the nervous system, whose channels are just as susceptible to capacity limits, equivocation and the degrading effects of 'noise', as are those of the telephone and radio.

Information Capacities of the Eye, Ear and Central Nervous System

The initial application of information theory to radio-communications dealt with measures of information transmission rates and the capacities of channels of communication, and this was reflected in the field of physiological psychology. Jacobsen (1950, 1951) compared the relative capacities of the eye and ear, and concluded that there was a factor of about 30 in favour of the eye on the basis of nerve fibres leading from the organs. However, when consideration was given to the efficiency with which an individual nerve fibre transmits information, Jacobsen found that the 900,000 optic nerve fibres each produced 5 bits per second, compared with a maximum of 0.33 bits per second for each of the 30,000 auditory fibres, giving a factor of nearly 500 in favour of the eye.

These results indicated a far higher rate of information transmission for the eye when compared with the ear, at least as far as the optic and auditory nerves are concerned. However, further research indicated that there was a restriction on the amount of information that could be transmitted through the central nervous system, and that central information processing would be subjected to an upper limit. The existence of such a limit implies that any information beyond the limit is lost; in information theory this loss is called equivocation.

The earliest experiments indicated that this capacity of the central nervous system was rather low. Hake and Garner (1951) required subjects to make judgements concerning the position of a pointer between two markers and found that the channel capacity for judgements of visual position was approximately 3.25 bits. In other words, they could accurately and consistently assign up to about 9 alternative positions on the scale , but as the number of positions they were required to estimate increased beyond 9 the subjects became less efficient. Similar results were obtained by Pollack (1952, 1953) for absolute judgements of auditory pitch. Subjects were asked to listen to a tone and assign a numeral to it. When only two or three tones were used the listeners never confused them, with four tones confusions were quite rare, but with five or more tones confusions were frequent. The upper limit was estimated to be 2.5 bits (6 alternatives).

It was soon realized that for one-dimensional judgements we rarely confuse 7 or so alternatives, and this seems to be a general limit on our capacity for such judgements. With multi-dimensional judgements, with a number of independently variable attributes, the capacity would be expected to increase. The position of a dot inside a square is clearly a two dimensional proposition. If we have a capacity of 3.25 bits for estimating intervals, as the Hake and Garner experiment indicated, and if we do this for two dimensions we should get 6.5 bits as our capacity for locating points in a square. In fact, the limit appears to be 4.6 bits or 25 alternative positions (Klemmer and Frick, 1953), rather than the 90 predicted from the uni-dimensional judgements. Pollack (1953) anticipated that for listeners asked to judge both the loudness (2.3 bits) and pitch (2.5 bits) there would be an augmenting effect so that the multi-dimensional judgement would raise the capacity to 4.8 bits. The limit is raised, but only to 3.1 bits (9 alternatives rather than the 28 anticipated). In fact, the largest channel capacity in these early studies was found to be 7.2 bits (150 alternatives) when Pollack and Ficks (1954) used 6 different acoustic variables in their multi-dimensional display.

These results led Travers (1967) to state that:

> ....as more dimensions are added there is a decreasing increment in the channel capacity of the multi-dimensional system. People are less accurate in any one dimension if they must judge more than one attribute at a time.

The data suggest that the amount of information which can be taken in on a single presentation of a display is probably quite limited - perhaps of the order of 10 bits.

Further, the general conclusion was that the channel capacity is ordinarily less than that estimated by Jacobsen (1951), perhaps as little as a tenth of the figures given, and that the information used is probably less than one tenth of one percent of the channel capacity of the sensory input.

Human Information Processing: The Single-channel Model

At this time there was good evidence to suppose that the information available from the senses far exceeds the limits of the central processing system. In addition, evidence was emerging from a series of experiments which indicated that sensory information fed into a central system for processing information, which was effectively a single channel system, in which information could be processed sequentially from only one source at a time.

The question was, as there clearly is a limit to the capacity of the central system, how does the system select which information to pay attention to and which to ignore? The formulation of the first complete theory of human information processing and selective attention by Broadbent (1958) attempted to provide an answer to this. The theory had obvious implications for anyone involved in producing teaching materials, particularly if those materials use a combination of senses, as is the case with many audio-visual aids. Broadbent's model was later developed by Travers (1964) who placed the research scientists and audio-visual designers at such opposite poles in their ideas concerning human information processing capacities.

Broadbent's original theory evolved from a series of experiments and techniques developed in the early 1950's. As with information theory, the main impetus for interest in this area was the tremendous rate of development of communication systems during the second world war. Colin Cherry's work in this field demonstrates the international and inter-disciplinary nature of this branch of psychology. Although he was an Englishman his major contribution was published as a result of research conducted at the Massachusetts Institute of Technology, and it appeared in the 'Journal of the Acoustical Society of America.' It was called 'Some experiments on recognition of speech with one and two ears' (1953) and used the technique known as 'shadowing'. Shadowing consists of playing a message into a set of headphones and asking the subject to repeat the words of the message, keeping pace with the presentation as far as possible. It is, in fact, a lot easier than it may seem, though the spoken words are slightly delayed behind those to which the subject is attending, and the voice tends to have a pronounced monotony. If the material being shadowed is of a complex nature the subject will invariably have very little idea of what it is about, even though every word has been recognized and repeated.

Cherry was concerned with what he chose to call the 'cocktail party effect', which also has the more scientific title: selective attention. He wanted to know how we were able to select that one voice to which we are attending from the general babble of the party. He was also interested in the retention of information from conversations to which we do not pay attention. In the experiments one continuous spoken message was fed into a headphone on the subject's left ear and a different message was applied to the right ear. The subject was then asked to repeat one of the messages concurrently while listening, and to make no mistakes. The really fascinating thing about the experiment concerns the nature of the subject's perception of the unattended message at the unshadowed ear. The subject could say little about it, apart from acknowledging that sounds occurred. In further experiments Cherry attempted to find out just what attributes of the rejected message were recognized.

In one experiment, for example, both messages started in English, and when the subject was comfortably shadowing the attended message, the unattended message was changed from English to German. When questioned later the subject was unaware of the change.

In another experiment the unattended message was composed of one of the following: normal English spoken by a male; English spoken by a female; English played in reverse; and, finally, a 400 cycle per second tone. With all the conditions of human speech, including the reversed speech, all subjects reported it as such, but could not identify specific words or even the language as English. Physical characteristics, such as a change to female voice or the introduction of the tone, were always noticed.

Cherry concluded from these experiments that detailed aspects such as language, individual words or semantic content are not noticed in the unattended channel. In effect, he felt that the utilization of information by the higher centres of the nervous system can be represented best by a single channel system. Broadbent extended this idea that the perceptual system generally functions as a single channel with information from only one source gaining access to it at a given time. But he cautioned against saying simply that 'a man cannot listen to two things at once'. On the contrary, he receives some information even from the unattended ear: but there is a limit to that amount of information. Broadbent (1954) had found that subjects could actually recall details of information presented to the unattended ear, under the specific conditions known as 'dichotic presentation'. Subjects were presented with three pairs of simultaneous digits, one of each pair to each ear (Figure 5-4), and were asked to recall as many digits as they could. Under normal circumstances subjects would have had little difficulty in remembering 7 or even 10 digits,

Figure 5-4. Dichotic listening experiment (Broadbent, 1954)

5	3	1	RIGHT EAR
6	4	2	LEFT EAR

Anticipated recall: 1,2,3,4,5,6 or 2,1,4,3,6,5

Actual recall : 1,3,5,2,4,6 or 2,4,6,1,3,5

Figure 5-5. Simplified version of Broadbent's Model of Information Flow (1958).

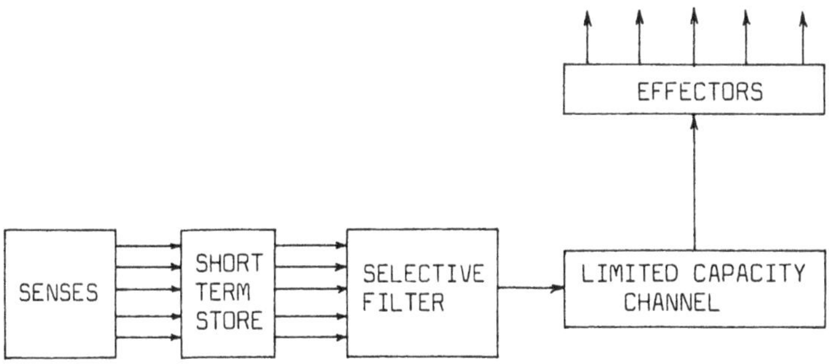

but under dichotic presentation they could recall only 4, 5 or 6.

The most interesting observation was that subjects preferred to report the digits by ear rather than in the order in which they were heard. In Figure 5-4, digits 1 and 2 are presented simultaneously, both being presented before the second set, digits 3 and 4. If subjects reported digits in temporal order both 1 and 2 would be recalled before either 3 or 4, giving two alternative temporal report patterns (anticipated). However, subjects chose to report the digits first by one ear and then by the other. When six pairs of digits were given, so that subjects had to recall 6 digits from one ear, before switching to the other, subjects were unable to recall the second set. Broadbent concluded that there must be a short-term memory store for information lying between the two stages of recognition of auditory messages. The experiment was repeated with half the digits presented to the ears and half to the eyes and the same result was obtained, showing that the buffer storage system was a general feature of human perception (Broadbent, 1956). This short-term memory store holds items which have not yet received attention and it may be thought of as keeping a record of raw sensory data. These results, and those of many other psychologists, physiologists and communications engineers, led Broadbent to the tentative formulation of his model of information flow in the human organism (Figure 5-5).

According to the Broadbent model, information passes from the senses and is held for a few seconds in the short term memory store where it will rapidly fade unless the selective filter mechanism permits access to the single limited channel, thence to the higher centres concerned with long term memory and control of behaviour.

The short-term store which feeds information into the processing channel, via the filter mechanism, was demonstrated to have certain limitations, in that only a relatively small number of items could be held in the memory at a given time, and that attention to new inputs causes old activations to fade away. Even short lists will completely fade in as little as 18 seconds if the subject is prevented from repeating the list to himself (a process known as 'rehearsal').

Beating the Channel Capacity: "Chunking" Information

The limit of the storage system is 6-10 units of information, and these units were called 'chunks' by Miller (1956) to differentiate them from 'bits', because the amount of information retained is not fixed. If the storage of items was like absolute judgement, then there should be a fixed amount of information that can be retained. We should remember less items when they contain a lot of information

Table 5-1. Ways of Recoding Sequences of Binary Digits.

Binary Digits (bits)		1 0 1 0 0 0 1 0 0 1 1 1 0 0 1 1 1 0
2:1	Chunks	10 10 00 10 01 11 00 11 10
	Recoding	2 2 0 2 1 3 0 3 2
3:1	Chunks	101 000 100 111 001 110
	Recoding	5 0 4 7 1 6
4:1	Chunks	1010 0010 0111 0011 10
	Recoding	10 2 7 3 2
5:1	Chunks	10100 01001 11001 110
	Recoding	20 9 25 6

Figure 5-6. Effects of Recoding Binary Digits on Short-Term Memory Performance.

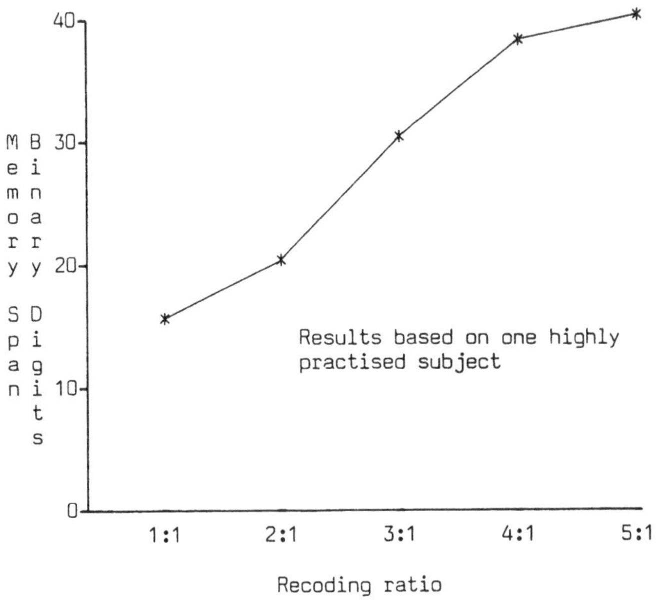

and remember more when they contain little information. As Miller pointed out:

> For example, decimal digits are worth 3.3 bits apiece. We can recall about 7 of them, for a total of 23 bits of information. Isolated English words are worth about 10 bits apiece. If the total amount of information is to remain constant at 23 bits, then we should be able to remember only 2 or 3 words chosen at random. (Miller, 1956, p.91)

Clearly, this is not the case, we can recall substantially the same number of items for a range of materials: digits, letters, words. In fact, by a process of coding and recoding information into larger chunks to increase the total amount of information, Miller demonstrated that the informational bottleneck, caused by the severe limitations placed on the amount of information that we are able to receive, process and remember, could be stretched. Strings of binary digits were recoded by experimental subjects who were trained to code the strings into increasingly more complex chunks (Table 5-1). This meant that a string of 20 binary digits could be reduced to just four chunks of information using re-coding techniques. This, in turn, permitted the amount of information held in short-term storage to be increased dramatically (Figure 5-6). Miller concluded from this data that 'The kind of linguistic recoding that people do seems to me to be the very lifeblood of the thought processes.' In other words, given the inherent limitations of our information processing system, we extend our capacities by recoding information in a more economical form, from which we can reconstitute the original message when required, much as we do with dried vegetables when shelf storage space is limited.

Human Information Processing: Alternative Models

Miller had demonstrated one way in which the basic limitations of the single-channel information processing system could be overcome and within a short time further research began to challenge a central concept of the Broadbent model, that unattended information could only be analyzed at the level of gross physical characteristics. For example, Moray (1959) found that although his subjects could not recall nor recognize irrelevant messages presented as many as 35 times to the unattended ear, they frequently heard their own name when presented in this channel.

Figure 5-7. Channel Switching.

Attended Ear : sitting at the mahogany / three
Unattended Ear: let us look at these / table

Further, Treisman (1960) demonstrated in an elegant fashion that subjects would follow the sense of a passage rather than the channel being shadowed, which indicated that processing was to some extent semantic. Figure 5-7 demonstrates how two sentences are switched in the shadowing experiment. Treisman found that subjects frequently shifted attention to the unattended ear to complete the sense of the sentence, so that it read 'sitting at the mahogany table', rather than 'sitting at the mahogany three'.

The conclusion from these experiments was that some, but not all, of the information from all the channels is

Figure 5-8. Treisman and Geffen's Attenuator Model of Attention.

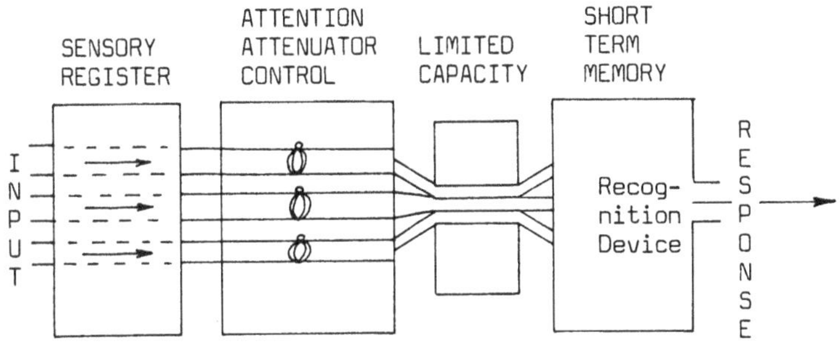

processed and this led to the development of Treisman and Geffen's (1967) 'attenuator' model of attention. Figure 5-8 shows how the model permits various sources to use the channel simultaneously. However, since there is a limited capacity, inputs from some channels must be attenuated.

This model has one primary channel that is being attended to, while all other channels are passing information in reduced amounts, but in such a way that whenever important information enters one of these attenuated channels it can be responded to. Treisman and Geffen (1967) obtained results strongly favouring this 'attenuation' view. Their subjects shadowed one of two dichotically presented prose passages, while simultaneously they had to monitor both channels for the occurrence of a target word, tapping each time it was detected. The results showed that whereas 90% of target words were identified in the primary channel, only about 9% were responded to in the unattended channel.

Norman (1968) extended this model of selection and attention to include a 'pertinence' factor (Figure 5-9). Pertinence, in the Norman model, is based on the expectations of future inputs and the properties of the currently attended channel of information. Certain classes of inputs, such as the sound of one's name, can be expected to have a permanently high level of pertinence, others will have levels which fluctuate with the expectations and analyses of ongoing events. The items in storage were termed 'logogens' by Morton (1969) in his complementary theoretical position. The logogens are seen as having thresholds, with the output for further processing depending on the level of activation from both sensory input processing and pertinence. Norman's model incorporates suggestions that for

Figure 5-9. Norman's Model of Selection and Attention.

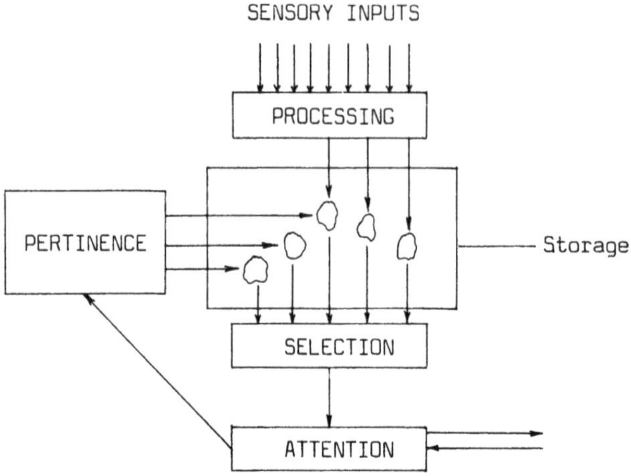

proper assessment all input information must have access to storage (Deutsch and Deutsch, 1963), and that an adjustable threshold pre-sensitizes the organism to sensory information of high relevance (Treisman and Geffen, 1967).

The item selected for further processing by the attention mechanism in the Norman model corresponds to the stored representation which received the greatest combination of pertinence and sensory activation. This was developed in a further paper by Norman and Bobrow (1975) who suggested that varying allocations of attention can be made up to the capacity limit of the processing system. An important distinction was made between resource limitations and data limitations. Resource limitations depend on the available internal resources of the human processor; data limitations relate to the sources of data forming the incoming signals. The suggestion was that some tasks require less than maximum processing resources and that if two tasks together required less than the maximum available they could both be performed simultaneously without any decrement in performance. However, if more than the maximum processing resources are required effort will be directed in favour of one or the other, resulting in a deterioration in the performance. The concept of data limitation introduces the constraints imposed by the external stimulus upon the processing system. With some tasks, applying more resources to processing may not result in an increase in performance.

The result is that the task has reached the point of pure data limitation. In such a case performance can only be improved by adjusting the stimulus data.

The Norman-Bobrow account resolved some anomalies in the data concerning information available in unattended channels and it is now generally accepted that information in these channels receives a level of processing higher than the crude physical characteristics suggested by the early Broadbent model. The processing is probably as high as semantic processing, and allows for channel switching as important information is registered in the attenuated channel. Cherry and Taylor (1954) demonstrated that this switching time was in the region of one sixth of a second or about 160-170 msecs, and Broadbent (1956) obtained a similar figure of 200 msecs in a later experiment.

The overall picture which emerges from these and similar studies of attention and information processing is one in which the major sense organs show great differences in their capacities for transmitting information, the eye being endowed with a greater number of nerve fibres, each of which is capable of transmitting more information than the corresponding auditory fibres. However, the transmitted information from the senses enters the central processing system which has a limited capacity. This limited capacity for information processing causes attention to be directed mainly towards one of several competing channels, the remaining channels being attenuated or receiving less than optimal processing but still receiving some high-level processing. Attention can be switched rapidly as important information is registered in the attenuated channels.

Depth of Processing and Mental Effort

Implicit in most of the early models of information processing was the division of memory into two parts: short-term memory (STM) and long-term memory (LTM), each with different characteristics but with both being essentially verbal storage systems. The distinction between STM and LTM has more recently given way to the view that memory should be viewed as an integral part of the whole information processing system, and that STM and LTM are merely artifacts of different 'depths of processing' (Craik and Lockhart, 1972). The different levels of processing range from shallow or physical analysis of a stimulus, to deep or semantic analysis. The depth of processing is defined in terms of the meaningfulness extracted from the stimulus rather than the number of analyses performed upon it. Information which is processed at a greater depth, which will be more meaningful than shallow processed information, will also be more memorable.

A typical experiment designed to demonstrate such an effect consists of having subjects perform different orienting tasks with a list of words before being given a recall test. Some tasks, such as detecting the occurrence of specific letters in the words or deciding the part of speech appropriate to each word, do not involve deep processing, whereas others, such as judging the pleasantness or frequency of usage, involve semantic processing at a deep level. Recall scores have generally tended to be higher for the deep processing list, although there is some circularity in the argument as to what constitutes a deep processing activity (Eysenck, 1984).

A recent adjunct to depth of processing is the elaboration of processing, with deep encodings being more elaborate or extensive and, therefore, providing more stored information than shallow processes. Retrieval, being affected by the amount of stored information, will be better for deep, elaborated encodings. Craik and Tulving (1975) ask 'Is spread of encoding a more satisfactory metaphor than depth?' and conclude that elaboration depends on the breadth of analysis carried out in each domain, and that a minimal semantic (deep) analysis will be more beneficial for memory than an elaborated structural (shallow) analysis.

Eysenck (1984) has suggested that a more complete theory than the original levels of processing proposed by Craik and Lockhart (1972) should take account of the fact that learning and memory depend upon at least four major factors: (1) the nature of the task (2) the nature of the stimulus materials (3) the characteristics of the subjects and (4) the nature of the retention test used.

Salomon (1984) has attempted to incorporate some of these factors into his application of the levels of processing theory in media research. He observed that while many U.S. experts claimed that television somehow inhibits 'deeper' processing of material and thus cannot serve well as an instructional medium, his cross-cultural study of Israeli and American children demonstrated that Israeli children retain more information and are more strongly affected by its formal features than their American peers. The Israeli children seemed to take the medium more seriously, processing the material with greater depth. He reasoned that above and beyond the cognitive activities a source of information activates or inhibits in learners (see Chapter 7), the depth with which its information is processed may depend on the way in which it is perceived. Pre-existing perceptions, particularly if socially reinforced, may preclude deep processing of available information.

In his experimental study he found that children thought of themselves as being more able to learn from tv than from books. When presented with similar material to learn from tv or print, the tv group reported investment of significantly less mental effort than the book group. This self-reported amount of invested mental effort (AIME) was reasoned to be related to 'non-automatic, effortful mental elaborations' which are at the base of both depth of processing and Langer's (1984) idea of mindfulness.

With more tv group members reporting the tv programme to be 'easy stuff' and more book children reporting the text to be 'difficult', it should follow that the tv group should perform better than the text group on the test measuring inference making and factual recognition. This was not the case. It was the text group that achieved significantly higher scores. Salomon found that for the book group those who felt more 'efficacious' tended to invest more mental effort in reading the text, and those who invested more mental effort learned more. A different pattern emerged for the tv group. Those who felt more efficacious tended to invest less mental effort in the programme and thus learned less from it. Measures of the perceived realism of the different media showed tv to be rated higher and this correlated with the perception that the message was easier and therefore demanded less effort, a worrying result for advocates of realism theories! These results clearly indicate the complexity of the inter-relationships between those factors suggested by Eysenck (1984) as impinging on applications of depth of processing and elaboration paradigms.

The Dual-coding Hypothesis

Although the depth of processing approach has attempted to resolve the STM/LTM division, a new division has emerged based on two different but complementary systems of storage: a semantic/verbal logogen system and an image-based 'imagen' system. This division is necessary because of increasing evidence in support of a separate image-based system of information storage.

Many researchers have found that pictures are superior to words in a variety of tasks. In fact, people have an extraordinary recognition memory for pictures, and one of the most dramatic demonstrations was reported by Shepard (1967). Subjects viewed 600 pictures and were tested for recognition by pairing one of these pictures together with a new picture, not previously seen by the subject, who was required to identify the picture from the original set. Words were also presented in a similar manner: one set made up from fairly common words (100 times or more per million according to Thorndike and Lorge, 1944); the other from 'rare' words (less than once per million). Finally, a third group had sentences presented in the same way. The medians of the percentage correct were 98.5, 90.0 and 88.2 for pictures, words and sentences. The results also indicated that subjects were better able to recognize words which were rare (92.5 percent correct) than when they were frequent (84.4 percent correct). Similar results have been found by Gorman (1961) and Olver (1965). Further results showing the extent of visual recognition memory were obtained by Standing, Conezio and Haber (1970), who presented 2,560 photographs for 10 seconds each over a period of 2 to 4 days, with recognition being maintained at 90.5 percent for as long as 3 days. When recognition time was reduced to one second per picture and the orientation of the picture in the test was altered, performance remained largely unimpaired. It has been suggested that the superiority of pictures in recognition tests may be due to differential verbal responses rather than 'picturability'. However, much of the evidence indicates a higher recognition memory for pictures of familiar objects than their concrete-noun labels (Paivio, 1971, p.183), indeed, recognition memory appears to be a direct function of stimulus concreteness: recognition increases from abstract words, to concrete words, to pictures.

Paivio (1971) has concluded that these results suggest both verbal and non-verbal symbolic processes. The superiority of concrete over abstract words suggests that referent images, associatively evoked by the concrete nouns, also facilitate recognition memory. Paivio also found that, within the limitations imposed by task characteristics, there is evidence that non-verbal processes can also play a crucial mediational role in free recall. 'Picturability' has been shown to be consistently positive since the earliest experiments (Kirkpatrick, 1894; Calkins, 1898) when average

Figure 5-10. Availability of two coding systems as a function of stimulus concreteness; degree of availability is indicated by the number of plus (+) signs.

STIMULUS	CODING SYSTEM	
	Imagery	Verbal
Picture	+++	++
Concrete word	+	+++
Abstract word	-	+++

recall was highest for objects and pictures when compared with words. Substantially the same results have been obtained in more recent time (Paivio, Rogers and Smythe, 1968; Sampson, 1970).

These results are of great interest because the required response in recall tasks is verbal in both cases (for both pictures and their verbal labels) and it may be anticipated that the to-be-remembered name should be more readily available when the stimulus is a word rather than a picture. Since it is not, verbal processes alone cannot account for the finding. On the basis of such experimental results Paivio has suggested the dual-coding model for pictures and words (Figure 5-10), where the availability of an item is indicated by its total representation in the dual (imagery/verbal) coding system.

Figure 5-11. Schematization of Paivio's Dual-coding Model (Bleasdale, 1983).

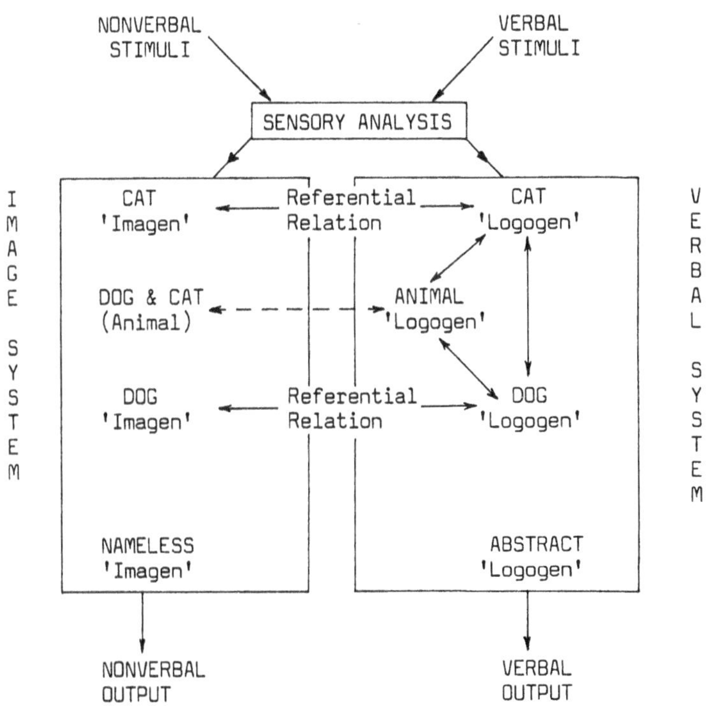

These results certainly indicate the presence of both a non-verbal (imagen) and a verbal (logogen) storage system. Indeed, Bleasdale (1983) claims that it would seem logical from a phylogenetic and ontogenetic perspective to assume that linguistic ability is preceded by the acquisition of perceptually-based information. Piaget (1953) suggested that knowledge structures (schemata) start to be formed almost from birth, and are basically formed from the co-ordinated remnants of sensory and motor signals that have been generated as the child has interacted with the world. This view has been incorporated by Paivio (1971), who also assumes that linguistic competence and performance are based on a substrate of imagery, although verbal behaviour and understanding ultimately becomes free of dependence not only upon a concrete situational context but to some extent from the imagery as well.

This concept of independent verbal and imaginal representational systems is at the heart of Paivio's dual-coding model (Figure 5-11). According to this model, words and pictures receive an initial, relatively peripheral, sensory analysis and are usually recognized by one of the stored representations (imagen/logogen), permitting access to further referential processing, during which time certain words may be imaged (especially concrete nouns) and pictures (or line drawings or objects) may be named. Finally, associative relations may be formed intraverbally among logogens and intra-imaginally among imagens.

Other models with similar dual-representational systems (Seymor, 1973; Morton, 1980), have also been developed to account for the accumulating evidence, coming from a wide variety of sources, for a separate image-related system.

WORDS, PICTURES AND INSTRUCTIONAL MEDIA

The pedagogical interest in the major channels of communication, their relative capacities, the limits placed on the processing of information, and the types of storage systems for processed information stems from a realization that the effectiveness of media generally, and instructional media in particular, will depend on the different properties of the channels used. Hsia (1968a) summarized these differences for the eye and ear and concluded that unless the fundamental information processing properties of the modalities are known then comparisons between different media using one or both senses will be meaningless (Table 5-1) and Travers (1967) agreed with this, clearly identifying those instructional tasks for which one or the other of the main channels is an obvious choice:

One cannot reasonably ask the general question whether

> the eye or the ear is more efficient for the transmission of information, for clearly some information is more efficiently transmitted by one sensory channel than by another. If a person needed to know about the appearance or physical characteristics of an unfamiliar animal he would do much better to examine the animal visually than to have a description related by another observer. Such visual observation would be best until he asked about the vocal noises emitted by the animal, in which case he would do better to hear the actual sound of the animal than to obtain visual information about the vocal mechanism. Where direct information is needed about the world, the sensory modality should be used which can best transmit directly the particular physical Information involved. (Travers, 1967, p.88)

Table 5-1: Channel Effectiveness (Hsia,H.J., 1968a).

AUDITORY CHANNEL	VISUAL CHANNEL
Temporal in nature	Spatial in nature, excepting tv and motion pictures
Sequential presentation	Both sequential and simultaneous presentation
Poor referability	Good referability: information can be stored in the display.
Fewer dimensions in information coding	Numerous dimensions in information coding
Greater flexibility; variation in connotations, nuances and inflection	Restricted flexibility and advanced coding
Rate of transmission limited to speaking rate	Much faster rate of transmission
Less versatility	Greater versatility
More attention demanding	Less attention demanding
More resistant to fatigue	Less resistant to fatigue

Words: Print and Speech

However, under certain circumstances it is quite legitimate to compare the efficiency of the two main sensory modalities because both may seem appropriate. For example, identical material may be presented to both eye and ear in the form of print or speech. Based on the knowledge gained from cognitive psychology it can be postulated that the eye with its superior capacity will be more effective, although the limiting factor in the form of the central processing capacity may diminish the eye's overall superiority. Also, auditory information may have a greater tendency to become data limited because of the lower transmission rate of the peripheral nervous pathways. This would suggest that for certain types of information the application of additional processing resources would not effect improvements in performance, which could only be brought about by changes in the stimulus data. Further, it could be argued that print will gain access to both verbal and image systems, enhancing memory performance.

Day and Beach (1950) conducted one of the earliest and most thorough surveys of the research literature comparing visual and auditory presentation of information, and reached the following conclusions:

1. Meaningful, familiar material is more efficiently presented aurally, whereas meaningless and unfamiliar material is more efficiently presented visually.
2. The greater the reading ability of the receiver, the relatively more effective is a visual presentation.
3. The relative efficiency of a visual presentation increases with age from a definite inferiority at the age of six to a possible superiority at the age of sixteen.
4. Unusually difficult material is more effectively received with a visual presentation, whereas particularly easy material is better understood with an auditory presentation. The relative effectiveness of the visual presentation increases with increasing difficulty of the material.
5. The relative efficiency of a visual presentation diminishes as the interval of delayed recall increases.

There is a tendency here to support the predictions made on the basis of the new understanding of human information processing. Performance was found to be dependent on age, reading skill and the difficulty of the material and this was confirmed for studies using nonsense syllables or digits, meaningful words in serial order, and meaningful prose reviewed by Hartman (1961a). He found that:

> Relative channel effectiveness depends on the difficulty or complexity of the material for a given group of subjects provided the subjects can read. With material such as nonsense syllables and digits, adults find print an advantage. The reading skills of younger children, however, are so limited that the audio channel is probably the most effective for them regardless of task. (Hartman, 1961a, p.237)

In other words, the print channel becomes more effective relative to the audio channel as the difficulty of material increases, provided a fair degree of literacy is present. The meaningful prose materials consisted of educational talks, passages selected from fiction, essays and advertisements. Print was found to be superior in nine studies; audio was favoured in eleven; and three found no difference. With few exceptions, those studies favouring print dealt with adult subjects and complex stimulus materials and the studies supporting the relative effectiveness of the audio channel used young children as subjects, or adults and older children with simpler information.

Gulo and Baron (1965) presented prose material via print, lecture, television lecture and radio to college students and found reading to be superior to the other three presentations on a multiple-choice retention test. Thalberg (1964) found that for moderately difficult and very difficult material, reading was superior to listening for college students. These results were confirmed by Levie and Dickie (1973) in their later review.

One explanation for the superiority of reading relates to the greater referability of print, first recognized by Day and Beach (1950), combined with the fact that during equated time periods in which listening subjects were receiving only one exposure, reading subjects (who were receiving information at a faster rate, because reading is faster than speaking) could obtain more than one learning opportunity by re-reading. The results are also consonant with estimates of the higher rate of information transmission within the visual system and the probable lower data limitation threshold of the auditory system.

Words: Comparisons of Multi-channel with Single-channel Presentations

Results of studies comparing information presented to one sense modality with that presented to more than one modality are of particular importance when considering the Broadbent (1958) model of information processing as elaborated by Travers (1967) for information transmission by means of audio-visual materials. In this model incoming information is compressed (redundancy is reduced) by the sense organs and peripheral nervous system so that some bits of information are 'chunked' together into fewer bits of information. This compressed information enters a central processing system which can handle sequential but not simultaneous information. If the central processing system is overloaded, some information may be stored briefly before it fades. The model predicts that if a presentation of the same information (spoken words and the same printed words), delivered simultaneously to both channels, is compared with either separately, no difference will be observed in the performance (recognition or recall) since all information must ultimately pass through a sequential processing system.

Later models, particularly those of Paivio (1971) and Morton (1980), support an alternative view of the results of such comparisons. A combination of spoken word and written word would activate both imagen and logogen systems, contributing to an increase in performance when compared with single presentations. Print alone would also have access to both systems, via the referential relation links, but not in such a direct manner.

The results of Day and Beach (1950) clearly support the later view. Another of their conclusions states unequivocally that a combined visual and auditory presentation leads to more efficient comprehension than either alone. Similarly, Hartman (1961a) reviewed nine studies comparing audio-print with print alone and found seven of them to favour the simultaneous presentation. Hartman (1961b) also found the audio-print presentation to be the most consistently effective of seven possible combinations of three channels tested. He concluded that a simultaneous audio-print presentation is more effective than either audio alone or print alone, when the simultaneously presented information is redundant (ie. when the same information is presented to both channels).

Van Mondfrans and Travers (1964), however, found evidence to support the Broadbent/Travers model. When recall of common words presented simultaneously by vision and audition was compared with words presented by vision alone and by audition alone no differences were found. Hsia (1968b) later found an audio-visual presentation of prose passages to be affected less than either audition or vision alone when 'noise' was introduced into the display (25% white noise in the audio channel; random black dots scattered over 25% of the visual display). Severin (1967) found that when recognition testing was provided in the channel or channels in which the information was presented, words presented simultaneously in audio and print were not significantly different from the print only condition, but were superior to the audio only presentation. Interestingly, the most effective condition was audio plus related pictures, which was superior to the print condition, a result consonant with the dual-coding model.

Joy and John Menne (1972) confirmed Hartman's conclusion. They tested their subjects under aural, visual and audio-visual presentations. Three simple four-line verses, each containing 22 words were presented via television. The subjects each received an audio presentation, a visual presentation and a combined presentation of words, spoken and written. After each they were required to recite the verse. The results demonstrated that an audio-visual presentation was superior to either presentation alone.

The weight of evidence is clearly in favour of the later models of human information processing, with their emphasis on resource allocation, data limitation and dual coding of information in separate but related image and verbal systems. These studies do represent a rather special case, with the same material (words) being presented to the two channels.

There are some limited pedagogical applications that may be derived from this work, for example, in the teaching of languages, but comparisons of pictures and words are of much greater educational interest. After all, the principle aim of the early educational media theorists was to set education free from the constraints imposed by 'excessive verbalism'.

Words and Pictures: Comparisons of Single-channel Presentations

There is a complication in this area because it opens up intra-channel comparisons, as well as inter-channel comparisons. Thus, we can consider differences between words and their pictorial representations within one channel (print and pictorial: visual channel) and between channels (spoken words and pictures: auditory and visual channels). Much of the research has concentrated on the intra-channel comparison.

Hartman (1961a), in his review, concluded that the weight of studies comparing a pictorial presentation with an audio presentation (eg. pictures of objects compared with spoken words of the objects), favoured the pictorial mode, although he was cautious in his commitment to the generalization because of the small number of studies, and because one of the studies compared the effectiveness of the visuals in films with their sound tracks, a procedure which compares two elements which may have substantially different functions within the display. The results do, however, confirm those obtained for spoken and printed words, which demonstrated superiority for the visual channel.

Comparisons between pictorial representations and written words have received much wider concern - the attraction of tighter experimental control is obviously one factor. Hartman (1961a) reported five such studies, all favouring the pictorial channel. Later studies (Gorman, 1961; Olver,1965; Rohwer, Lynch, Levin and Suzuki, 1967; Jenkins, Neale and Deno, 1967; Shepard, 1967) confirmed this in a variety of situations. Recall and recognition have been shown to increase from abstract words, to concrete words, to pictures, leading to Paivio's proposal for the dual-coding approach to perception and cognition.

Paivio (1971) describes one experiment in which subjects were shown words or pictures for a fraction of a second and were then asked to recall them. One group was tested after a delay of one week. Half of the subjects were not informed of the recall test until after the presentation ('incidental' group) . The stimulus items were composed of pictures, concrete words (ie. the words associated with the pictures) and abstract words. The immediate recall results demonstrated a clear advantage for pictures, with concrete words superior to abstract words, for both 'incidental' and 'intentional' groups. The delayed responses maintained this order, with the incidental group showing a higher delayed recall of pictures than was previously obtained for concrete words on immediate testing. Needless to say, this and many other studies led eventually to the development of the later models of human information processing.

Words and Pictures: Comparisons of Multi-channel with Single-channel Presentations

This strikes at the very heart of audio-visual theory. What evidence is there to support the idea that a combination of audio and visual will bring about more complete learning than either channel alone?

In most of the early studies information presented to the two channels was related (eg. a pictorial representation of an object and a verbal description of it) although other possibilities do exist: the information may be unrelated or even contradictory. Hartman's (1961a) review found the available thirteen studies to be inadequate for the formulation of generalizations, but did conclude that comparisons of pictorial-verbal presentations with single-channel presentations strongly indicated an advantage for the combination of channels.

Early researches dealing with motion film variables (Hoban and Van Ormer, 1950) supported the advantage for sound plus picture combinations, and this was confirmed by

Ketcham and Heath (1962) who demonstrated that sound plus relevant pictures was superior to sound alone, with sound plus irrelevant pictures proving to be least effective. When comparing the effectiveness of relevant pictures in multiple-channel communication Severin (1967) found audio plus related pictures to be the most successful of six combinations, including print alone and audio alone, with unrelated-picture/audio combinations least effective. More recently, Nugent (1982) demonstrated that when content is the same in visual, audio and print channels, younger students learn equally well from all modes, but combining pictures with print or audio generally maximized learning. This research suggests that by conveying information through both linguistic and iconic symbols students were provided with complementary processing systems, and they could alternate between the two to obtain information. This study offers support for the theoretical position that learners process pictorial and linguistic information through functionally independent, though interconnected, cognitive systems.

The most thorough exploration of multiple-channel communication has been undertaken by Dwyer (1978). In a series of experiments starting in 1967 Dwyer systematically studied the effects of different conditions of presentation of the same material. This consisted of a study unit 'The Human Heart', which was presented either as an oral/verbal presentation, with the recorded script being accompanied by keys words in the visual display, or as an illustrated presentation, with pictures accompanying the recorded script. Several different series of pictures were prepared, ranging from simple line drawings to full colour photographs. In addition to different types of illustration, there were four different types of test: a drawing test, in which the subject drew a labelled representative diagram of the heart; an identification test, in which subjects had to identify certain numbered parts of a heart; a terminology test which evaluated knowledge of specific terms; and a comprehension test which evaluated understanding and an ability to use information to explain phenomena. The individual scores were pooled to give a 'total criterial score', showing the subject's total knowledge and understanding.The results of the first experiment led Dwyer to conclude that:

> The results of this study indicate that when students viewed their respective instructional presentations for equal amounts of time, the simple line drawing presentation was significantly more effective in facilitating achievement than was the oral presentation without visuals on the drawing, identification and total criterial tests. The oral presentation without visuals

> of the heart was found to be as effective as each of the visually complemented treatments on both the terminology and comprehension tests. (Dwyer, 1972, p.22)

The results have not always been quite so clear-cut. With different populations of subjects the results have sometimes shown visuals to be beneficial for the terminology and comprehension tests. Visuals produce consistently higher levels of achievement for the drawing, terminology and total criterial test, when compared with the oral presentation, although such benefits are not sustained over a two week delayed-testing period. However, Dwyer's research consistently demonstrates the benefits associated with pictorial accompaniments to spoken commentaries, and provides additional support to the audio-visual theorists.

Texts and Illustrations

The effects of illustrations on the understanding of text is obviously of pedagogic interest. It is assumed that illustrations must add to recall, comprehension and understanding. Otherwise, why should publishers of school exts take so much trouble to prepare them? However, despite this assumption, much of the early research on text illustrations reported a slight advantage for text alone (Miller, 1938; Vernon, 1953, 1954) and this led Samuels in 1970 to conclude that pictures do not facilitate comprehension of text. He was particularly concerned that the assumed benefits of illustrations produced to supplement texts should be subjected to scrutiny, claiming that:

> If fish were to become scientists, the last thing they might discover would be water. Similarly, researchers have too often failed to investigate important aspects of their environment because being immersed in it, they fail to notice certain components of it; or, having noticed a component, they simply assume it must be that way. One such example from reading is the ubiquitous use of illustrations.... (Samuels, 1970, p.397)

Samuels suggested that pictures are used in instructional materials under the assumption that they facilitate learning by appealing directly to the student's five senses. This was tested for by Bourisseau, Davis and Yamamoto (1965) but, as with other studies reviewed by Samuels, the results were negative and the authors concluded that although many people believed that one picture is worth a thousand words, so far as sensory response is concerned, the assumption is unwarranted.

In conclusion Samuels suggested that the answer to the

question 'Should pictures be used as adjuncts to printed texts?' depended on the objectives.

> If the objective is to promote acquisition of a sight vocabulary, the answer would seem to be 'no.' If the objective is to facilitate comprehension, the answer is less definite.... Although the research, in general, does not show that pictures aid comprehension, neither does it show that they hinder comprehension (Samuels, 1970, p.405)

Much subsequent research disagrees with this view, but the out-of-date reviews may still be sighted authoritatively as sources of wisdom concerning this topic, according to Levie and Lentz (1982). Having 'discovered water' later researchers began to analyze the constituent parts and determine how they interacted.

Levie and Lentz (1982) reviewed the later research, starting by looking at the effect of visual illustrations on the learning of verbal information presented in the text. This excluded oral or audio-visual presentations; word lists, single sentences, or deliberately ambiguous passages; charts, diagrams and graphs. Essentially they were looking at studies comparing learning from illustrated texts versus learning from text alone. They took what they termed an 'information-analysis approach' to the research, based on the possible relationships between the information in a text passage and in the illustrations. Information presented only in the text passage (ie. without illustration) they termed 'non-illustrated text information'; other information provided only in the pictures was termed 'picture-only information'; and when text material was accompanied by relevant illustrations it was called 'illustrated text information.'

The researcher's test of learning is a critical factor in evaluating results in this area. For example, does the test measure the learning of illustrated text information only, non-illustrated text information only, or some combination? Levie and Lentz (1982) claimed that when researchers control these relationships, greater clarity about the effects of text illustrations is possible. They identified a total of 46 comparisons of learning illustrated text information from illustrated text versus text alone. A majority of the results were statistically significant and in favour of the illustrated text, giving an average effect size of 0.55, with the illustrated text group score averaging 36% more than the text alone. This led Levie and Lentz to conclude that:

> With a few exceptions, the results showed that illustrations had a significant positive effect on

> learning illustrated text information and no effect on learning non-illustrated text information. (Levie and Lentz, 1982, p.198)

Vernon (1953) suggested that illustrations laid undue emphasis on certain points and therefore distracted attention from other aspects of the text, thus hindering overall performance. A more popular view is that illustrations have a generalized motivating effect and will improve learning of information which is not illustrated. Levie and Lentz (1982) lend support to the middle view, that illustrations simply have no effect on learning non-illustrated text information.

When learning a combination of illustrated and non-illustrated text information it can be predicted from the above results that the effect of including illustrations will depend on the proportion of supported text in the test employed. This is confirmed by Levie and Lentz, who indicate that 'the addition of pictures should not be expected to hinder learning; nor should pictures always be expected to facilitate learning.' However, they conclude that learning is better with pictures in most cases.

Dwyer's researches include many studies in which the materials are presented in the form of a text, and the results of these were also analyzed by Levie and Lentz. Similar differential effects were observed for the different types of test as were found in the studies using an audio-visual presentation, with the largest effect size in favour of illustrations being observed for the drawing test (0.58), lesser effects for the identification test (0.38) and terminology test (0.28), and a trivial effect for the comprehension test (0.09). These results were interpreted as showing that the degree to which an educational objective is aided by pictures depends on the emphasis given to knowledge about spatial information in the test of learning, demonstrating a consistency between Dwyer's work and other research in this area.

Levie and Lentz's results have been confirmed in a further meta-analysis conducted by Levin, Anglin and Carney (1987). Levin (1981) had previously speculated that illustrations could be categorized as having five different functions: decoration, representation, organization, interpretation and transformational. He suggested that each of these functions would produce different degrees of prose learning facilitation, ranging from no effect for the decorative function to substantial for transformational pictures designed specifically with a mnemonic objective in mind. Moderate to substantial facilitation was anticipated for representation, organization and interpretation functions. The meta-analysis confirmed these expectations with a near zero effect size for decorative illustrations and an average 0.71 across other text-relevant studies. For children the average effect size ranged from 0.5 for representational pictures to 1.43 for transformational illustrations; for older subjects the range was from 0.7 to 1.04. These results further confirm the power of illustrations to enhance prose learning, particularly when pictorial information is further encoded as in the transformational mode.

Pictorial Complexity

Levie and Lentz (1982) comment that even within the limits imposed on studies considered in their review there is still considerable diversity, particularly in the types of illustration used, which varied from simple line drawings to colour photographs. Dwyer's work demonstrated advantages for including illustrations compared with no illustrations for specific types of test, offering support to the audio-visual approach, but as yet the differential effects of the various types of illustrations included in his researches have not been discussed. Four different types of illustration were used in most of Dwyer's experiments. They varied in the amount of detail and general pictorial complexity, and were produced in a black and white version and a colour version, giving a total of eight different types which could be arranged, according to Dwyer, along a 'realism continuum' (Figure 5-12).

Figure 5-12. Dwyer's realism continuum for black and white and coloured illustrations.

1. Simple line representations (black and white)
2. Simple line representations (colour)
3. Drawings - detailed and shaded (black and white)
4. Drawings - detailed and shaded (colour)
5. Photographs of a model (black and white)
6. Photographs of a model (colour)
7. Photographs of a real heart (black and white)
8. Photographs of a real heart (colour)

Dwyer (1978) suggested that the two competing theories of human information processing, represented by the single-channel and multiple-channel perspectives, predicted different results for experiments varying the degree of realism in illustrations. The multiple-channel theorists, which Dwyer identified as stemming from the writings of Dale (1946) and Carpenter (1953), predicted an increase in the efficiency in facilitating learning as the realism increased from the simple line representations to the photographs of a real heart. The single-channel theorists, based on the work of Broadbent (1958) and Travers (1964), predicted no effect from the increase in pictorial complexity, indeed when information in picture and text was redundant they predicted no effect from the addition of illustrations to the text. The results of the initial experiment (Dwyer, 1967) was equivocal. Illustrations did facilitate achievement for a majority of the test measures. However, increasing the degree of realism in the illustrations did not increase the performance on any of the tests. In other words, the addition of a simple line drawing enhanced performance on three of the five tests, but there was no difference in the effects of any of the different types of illustrations.

Further experiments reported by Dwyer (1972) tended to support the initial findings with a majority of the studies demonstrating superiority for the presentations illustrated with simple line drawings when assessed on the total criterial test and the drawing test. For the terminology and comprehension tests illustrations were generally not an advantage; and the identification test indicated an intermediate position, with many studies indicating benefits from the addition of simple line illustrations, and similar numbers indicating no such advantage. In only a minority of cases (16%) were illustrations which were more complex than the simple line drawings more effective, and there was no discernible pattern to this minor effect.

These results are not surprising when considered against the background of several decades of research in this area. Vandermeer (1954) had investigated the comparative effects of colour and black and white motion films, on the assumption that colour would add realism to the visual display, which would increase the efficiency of the films as teaching aids. This was not the case, and he concluded that:

> The use of colour in instructional films which may seem to 'call for colour' does not appear to be justified in terms of the greater learning on the part of those who view the films. If colour is to be used effectively in films there must be careful pre-production consideration of the probable psychological impact of specific uses of colour upon the learner. (Vandermeer, 1954, p.134)

These results were confirmed by later researchers (eg. Kanner and Rosenstein, 1960) and reviews (Kanner, 1968; Cox, 1976).

A fascinating report from the Yale film research programme (May and Lumsdaine, 1958) showed the lack of effects from increased pictorial complexity when they compared a crude black and white film version of a film, based on the story-board sketches, with the finished full colour motion picture. The results were totally unexpected: there was no difference in the achievement of the objectives between the two versions, although there was a large difference in cost. Twyford (1954) had obtained similar results when comparing a full colour motion picture with a version consisting of a series of still pictures in black and white. There were slight differences in favour of the expensive colour version, but the differences obtained were not of educational significance, and Twyford cautioned against the indiscriminate use of realistic presentations when they could not be justified in terms of instructional benefits.

Human Information Processing: Conclusions

There has been a healthy rivalry between theorists advocating either a single-channel of limited capacity or a multi-channel approach to human information processing. The present position calls for a resolution of the different positions. In part, both positions are correct.

The single-channel theory proposed by Broadbent (1958) and elaborated by Travers (1967) is no longer wholly tenable, and it is reasonable to assume that varying allocations of attention can be made to incoming information, with apparently unattended information receiving high levels of processing, as suggested by Norman and Bobrow (1975). Incoming information may receive variable amounts of processing, and the depth of processing may depend upon such factors as the 'realism' of the display, the receiver's perceived self-efficacy and the perceived demand characteristics of the particular medium.

There is good evidence to support two complementary representation systems, along the lines suggested by Paivio (1971), with extensive interconnections between verbal and image systems. This is clearly acceptable to the multi-channel advocates, and supports the early claims of the 'audio-visual' approach to educational technology.

However, there are limits to the audio-visual approach. Although multi-sensory presentations do seem to facilitate learning on specific tests, they do so only in circumstances where audio and visual components are mutually supportive. Visuals increase learning when they are relevant to the text or commentary, they do not produce a generalized effect on unrelated textual or verbal information. Visual information also appears to be compressed by the processing system, as suggested by Travers (1964). This is necessary because of the limited capacity of the system and precludes any facilitating effects anticipated by increasing pictorial complexity or realism. It suggests that for the more common activities associated with visual testing (eg. drawing, identifying) students may benefit from visuals which are pre-compressed and simplified by the instructor.

REFERENCES

Attneave, F. (1959) _Applications of Information Theory to Psychology_. New York: Holt-Dryden.

Bleasdale, F. (1983) 'Paivio's dual-coding model of meaning revisited'. In J.C. Yuille (Ed) _Imagery, Memory and Cognition_. New Jersey: Lawrence Erlbaum.

Bourisseau, W., Davis, O.L. and Yamamoto, K. (1965) 'Sense impression responses to differing pictorial and verbal stimuli', _Audio Visual Communication Review_, 13, 249-254.

Broadbent, D.E. (1954) 'Role of auditory localization and attention in memory span', _Journal of Experimental Psychology_, 47, 191-196.

Broadbent, D.E. (1956) 'Successive responses to simultaneous stimuli', _Quarterly Journal of Experimental Psychology_, 8, 145-152.

Broadbent, D.E. (1958) _Perception and Communication_. Oxford: Pergamon Press.

Calkins, M.W. (1898) 'Short studies in memory and in association from the Wellesley College psychological laboratory', _Psychological Review_, 5, 451-462.

Carpenter, C.R. (1953) 'A theoretical orientation for instructional film research', _Audio Visual Communication Review_, 1, 38-52.

Cherry, E.C. (1953) 'Some experiments on the recognition of speech, with one and two ears', _Journal of the Acoustical Society of America_, 25, 975-979.

Cherry, E.C. and Taylor, W.K. (1954) 'Some further experiments on the reception of speech, with one and two ears', _Journal of the Acoustical Society of America_, 26, 554-559.

Cox, S. (1976) 'Colour in learning from film and tv: a survey of the research with some indications for future investigations', _Educational Broadcasting International_, (June.)

Craik, F.M. and Tulving, E. (1975) 'Depth of processing and retention of words in episodic memory', _Journal of Experimental Psychology: General_, 104, 208-294.

Craik, F.I.M. and Lockhart, R.S. (1972) 'Levels of processing: a framework for memory research', _Journal of Verbal Learning and Verbal Behaviour_, 11, 671-684.

Dale, E. (1946) _Audiovisual Methods in Teaching_. London: Holt, Rinehart and Winston.

Dale, E. (1954) _Audiovisual Methods In Teaching (2nd Edition)_. London: Holt, Rinehart and Winston.

Day, W.F. and Beach, B.R. (1950) _A Survey of the Research_

Literature Comparing the Visual and Auditory Presentation of Information. Air Force Technical Report 5921, Contract No. W33- 039- AC-21269. Charlottesville: University of Virginia.

Deutsch, J.A. and Deutsch, D. (1963) 'Attention: some theoretical considerations', Psychological Review, 70, 80-90.

Dwyer, F.M. (1967) 'Adapting visual illustrations for effective learning', Harvard Educational Review, 37, 250-263

Dwyer, F.M. (1972) A Guide for Improving Visualized Instruction. State College, Pennsylvania: Learning Services.

Dwyer, F.M. (1978) Strategies for Improving Visual Learning. State College, Pennsylvania: Learning Services.

Eysenck, M.W. (1984) A Handbook of Cognitive Psychology. London: Erlbaum

Gibson, J.J. (1954) 'A theory of pictorial perception', Audio Visual Communication Review, 2(1), 3-23.

Gorman, A.M. (1961) 'Recognition memory for nouns as a function of abstractness and frequency', Journal of Experimental Psychology, 61,23-29.

Gulo, E.V. and Baron, A. (1965) 'Classroom learning of meaningful prose by college students as a function of sensory mode of stimulus presentation', Perceptual and Motor Skills, 21, 183- 186.

Hake, H.W., and Garner, W.R. (1951) 'The effect of presenting various numbers of discrete steps on scale reading accuracy', Journal of Experimental Psychology, 42, 358-366.

Hartman, F.R. (1961a) 'Single and multiple channel communication: a review of research and a proposed model', Audio Visual Communication Review. 9, 235-262.

Hartman, F.R. (1961b) 'Recognition learning under multiple channel presentation and testing conditions', Audio Visual Communication Review, 9, 24-43.

Hoban, C.F. and Van Ormer, E.B. (1950) Instructional Film Research 1918-1950. Technical Report No. SDC-269-7-19 Port Washington, New York: Special Devices Centre, Office of Naval Research.

Hsia, H.J., (1968a) 'On channel effectiveness', Audio Visual Communication Review, 16, 245-267.

Hsia, H.J., (1968b) 'Effects of noise and difficulty level of input information in auditory, visual, and audio-visual information processing', Perceptual and Motor Skills, 26, 99-105.

Jacobsen, H. (1950) 'The information capacity of the human ear', Science, 112, 143-144.

Jacobsen, H. (1951) 'The informational capacity of the human eye', Science, 113, 292-293.

Jenkins, J.R., Neale, D.C., and Deno, S.L. (1967) 'Differential memory for picture and word stimuli', Journal of Educational Psychology, 58, 303-307.

Jonassen, D.H. (1985) 'Learning strategies: a new educational technology', Programmed Learning and Educational Technology, 22(1), 26-34.

Kanner, J.H. (1968) The instructional effectiveness of colour television: a review of the evidence. Stanford University: Stanford, California. Ed 015 675

Kanner, J.H. and Rosenstein, A.J. (1960) 'Television in army training: colour versus black and white', Audio Visual Communication Review, 8, 243-252.

Ketcham, C.H. and Heath, R.N. (1962) 'Teaching effectiveness of sound with pictures that do not embody the material being taught', Audio Visual Communication Review, 10, 89-93.

Kirkpatrick, E.A. (1894) 'An experimental study of memory', Psychological Review, 1, 602-609.

Klemmer, E.T., and Frick, F.C. (1953) 'Assimilation of information from dot and matrix patterns', Journal of Experimental Psychology, 45, 15-19.

Knowlton, J.Q. (1966) 'On the definition of a picture', Audio Visual Communication Review, 14, 157-183.

Langer, E.J. (1984) 'Playing the Middle Against Both Ends: The Influence of Adult Cognitive Activity as a Model for Cognitive Activity in Childhood and Old Age.' In S.R. Yussen (Ed) The Development of Reflection. New York: Academic Press.

Levie, W.H. and Dickie, K.E. (1973) 'The Analysis and Application of Media'. In Travers, R.M.W. (Ed), Second Handbook of Research on Teaching. Chicago: Rand McNally.

Levie, W.H. and Lentz, R. (1982) 'Effects of text illustrations: a review of research' Educational Communication and Technology Journal, 30, 195-232.

Levin, J.R. (1981) 'On the Function of Pictures in Prose'. In F.J. Pirozzolo and M.C. Wittrock (Eds) Neuropsychological and Cognitive Processes in Reading. New York: Academic Press.

Levin, J.R., Anglin, G.J. and Carney, R.N. (1987) 'On Empirically Validating Functions of Pictures in Prose'. In D.A. Willow and H.A. Houghton (Eds) The Psychology of Illustration (Vol.1). London: Springer-Verlag.

May, M.A. and Lumsdaine, A.A. (1958) Learning from Films. Yale University Press: New Haven

Menne, J.M., and Menne, J.W. (1972) 'The relative efficiency of bimodal presentation as an aid to learning', Audio Visual Communication Review, 20, 170-180.

Miller, G.A. (1956) 'The magical number seven, plus or minus two: some limits on our capacity for processing information', Psychological Review, 63, 81-97.

Miller, G.A. and Frick, F.C. (1949) 'Statistical behaviouristics and sequences of responses', Psychological Review, 56, 311- 324.

Miller, W.A. (1938) 'Reading with and without pictures', Elementary School Journal, 38, 676-682.
Moray, N. (1959) 'Attention in dichotic listening', Quarterly Journal of Experimental Psychology, 11, 56-60.
Morris, C.W. (1946) Signs, Language and Behaviour. New York: Prentice-Hall
Morton, J. (1969) 'The interaction of information in word recognition', Psychological Review, 76, 175-178.
Morton, J. (1980) 'The logogen model and orthographic structure'. In U. Frith (Ed) Cognitive Processes in Spelling. London: Academic Press.
Norman, D.A. (1968) 'Toward a theory of memory and attention', Psychological Review, 75, 522-536.
Norman, D.A. and Bobrow, D.G. (1975) 'On data-limited and resource-limited processes', Cognitive Psychology, 7, 44-64.
Nugent, G. (1982) 'Pictures, audio, and print: symbolic representation and effect on learning', Educational Communication and Technology Journal, 30, 163-174.
Olver, M.A. (1965) 'Abstractness, Imagery, and Meaningfulness in Recognition and Free Recall.' Unpublished Master's Thesis, University of Western Ontario. Quoted in A. Paivio (1971) Imagery and Verbal Processes. New York: Holt, Rinehart and Winston.
Paivio, A. (1971) Imagery and Verbal Processes. New York: Holt, Rinehart and Winston.
Paivio, A., Rogers, T.B. and Smythe, P.C. (1968) 'Why are pictures easier to recall than words?', Psychonomic Science, 11, 137-138.
Piaget, J. (1953) The Origins of Intelligence in the Child. London : Routledge and Kegan Paul.
Pollack, I. (1952) 'The information of elementary auditory displays', Journal of the Acoustical Society of America, 24, 745-749.
Pollack, I. (1953) 'The information of elementary auditory displays II', Journal of the Acoustical Society of America, 25, 765-769.
Pollack, I., and Ficks, L. (1955) 'The information of elementary multi-dimensional auditory displays', Journal of the Acoustical Society of America', 26, 155-158.
Rohwer, W.D., Lynch, S., Levin, J.R. and Suzuki, N. (1967) 'Pictorial and verbal factors in the efficient learning of paired associates', Journal of Educational Psychology, 58, 278-284.
Salomon, G. (1984) 'Television is easy and print is tough: the differential investment of mental effort in learning as a function of perceptions and attributions', Journal of Educational Psychology, 76, 647-658.
Sampson, J.R. (1970) 'Free recall of verbal and non-verbal stimuli', Quarterly Journal of Experimental Psychology, 22, 215-221.

Samuels, S.J. (1970) 'Effects of pictures on learning to read, comprehension and attitudes', Review of Educational Research, 40, 397-407.

Severin, W.J. (1967) 'The effectiveness of relevant pictures in multiple-channel communications', Audio Visual Communication Review, 15, 386-401.

Seymour, P.H. (1973) 'A model for reading, naming, and comprehension', British Journal of Psychology, 64, 35-49.

Shannon, C.E. and Weaver, W. (1949) The Mathematical Theory of Communication. Urbana: University of Illinois Press.

Shepard, R.N. (1967) 'Recognition memory for words, sentences and pictures', Journal of Verbal Learning and Verbal Behaviour, 6, 156-163.

Standing, L., Conezio, J. and Haber, R.N. (1970) 'Perception and memory for pictures: single trial learning of 2,500 visual stimuli', Psychonomic Science, 19, 73-74.

Thalberg, P.S. (1964) An Experimental Investigation of the Relative Efficiency of the Auditory and Visual Modes of Presentation of Verbal Material. Doctoral dissertation, State University of Iowa. Ann Arbor, Michigan: University Microfilms, No. 64-7949.

Thorndike, E.L. and Lorge, I. (1944) The Teacher's Word Book of 30,000 Words. New York: Bureau of Publications. Teachers College.

Travers, R.M.W. (1964) 'The transmission of information to human receivers', Audio Visual Communication Review, 12, 373-385.

Travers, R.M.W. et al. (1964) Research and Theory Related to Audiovisual Information Transmission. Project No. 3-20-003. U.S. Department of Health, Education and Welfare, Office of Education.

Travers, R.M.W. et al. (1967) Research and Theory Related to Audiovisual Information Transmission, Revised Edition. Project No. 3-20-003. U.S. Department of Health, Education, and Welfare, Office of Education.

Treichler, D.G. (1967) 'Are you missing the boat in training aids?', Film and AV Communication, 1, 14-16.

Treisman, A.M. (1960) 'Contextual cues in selective listening', Quarterly Journal of Experimental Psychology, 12, 242-248.

Treisman, A.M. and Geffen, G. (1967) 'Selective attention: perception or response?', Quarterly Journal of Experimental Psychology, 19, 1-16.

Twyford, L.C., Davis, J.S. and Seitz, C.P. (1954) Evaluation of the Film: Military Police Support in Emergencies (Riot Control). Technical Report No. SDC 269-7-52. Instructional Film Program. Naval Training Devices Centre; Office of Naval Research: Port Washington-New York.

Van Mondfrans, A.P. and Travers, R.M.W. (1964) 'Learning of redundant material presented through two sensory modalities', Perceptual and Motor Skills, 19, 743-751.

Vandermeer, A.W. (1954) 'Colour vs black and white in instructional films', *Audio Visual Communication Review*, 2, 121-134.

Vernon, M.D. (1953) 'The value of pictorial illustration', *British Journal of Educational Psychology*, 23, 180-187.

Vernon, M.D. (1954) 'The instruction of children by pictorial illustration', *British Journal of Educational Psychology*, 24, 171-179.

CHAPTER 6

CONSTRUCTING REALITY

Eysenck (1984) has suggested that experimental psychology has increasingly become synonomous with cognitive psychology and identifies Broadbent's 'Perception and Communication' (1958) and Neisser's 'Cognitive Psychology' (1967) as being seminal influences on the 'booming, buzzing confusion that is contemporary cognitive psychology.'

Neisser (1976), in turn, identifies the developmental studies of Piaget as offering an alternative to earlier behaviouristic models of human behaviour, claiming that 'human nature is too important to be left to the behaviourists....' (p.8). Central to Neisser's position is the concept of the schema, which has been developed extensively by Piaget.

> Although perceiving does not change the world, it does change the perceiver. (So does action, of course.) The schema undergoes what Piaget calls 'accommodation,' and so does the perceiver. He has become what he is by virtue of what he has perceived (and done) in the past; he further creates and changes himself by what he perceives and does in the present. 'Existence precedes essence,' as the existentialists say. (Neisser, 1976, p.53)

Jonassen (1985) sees the present situation as a shift from a behaviouristic, mechanistic psychology of human behaviour to that of an active, constructive psychology, with learners viewed as organized entities actively constructing their own reality. He sees Piaget's theory of cognitive development as being of major importance to the new educational technologies, particularly Piaget's dictum that knowing is a process of constructing systems of transformations that model reality and that mature 'operational' thought is the product of:

> successive constructions, and the principal factor in this constructivism is an equilibration achieved by autoregulations that make it possible to remedy momentary incoherences, to resolve problems, and to surmount crises or periods of imbalance by a constant elaboration of fresh structures.... (Piaget, 1971, p.40)

PIAGET'S CONSTRUCTIVISM

Piaget rarely directed his attention specifically to education. Primarily he considered himself to be a biologist and a genetic epistemologist, indeed, he never really left biology even when he was so occupied with cognition.

For many years Piaget studied the water-snail, Limnaea stagnalis, which in tranquil water has an elongated shell. When moved to lakes where waves beat upon its shell, Piaget found that the young snail changes its shape, it contracts the muscles attaching it to rocks each time a wave breaks and eventually it becomes globular in shape. In time the snail's adaptation to the turbulent waters tends to become hereditary. Piaget moved some back to his aquarium where they retained their globular shape for many generations. For Piaget this is an example of how organisms may adapt genetically to novel surroundings. He does not fully subscribe to the Lamarkian heresy of the inheritance of acquired characteristics, but he disagrees with neo-Darwinian theory which sees organisms as essentially passive and dependent on chance mutation for adaptive change in the fight for survival. For Piaget, the adaptation is a dynamic, on-going process in which the hereditary structure of the organism interacts with the external environment in such a way as to reconstitute itself for better survival. Piaget (1971) identifies Waddington's (1957) theory of genetic assimilation as providing a basis for the mechanism by which such adaptive changes become genetically transmitted. This has led to Piaget's emphasis on the process that brings about progressive states of equilibrium: the dynamic, on-going self-regulating process which he calls equilibration.

His theory of cognitive development was presented in more than a hundred books and articles spanning more than fifty years. Many educationalists have been inspired by these writings, though Piaget has frequently pointed out that his ideas have not always been fully understood by such educationalists. Piaget's book 'The Science of Education and the Psychology of the Child' (1971) represents the fullest account of his thoughts on education. However, in order to understand these writings it is necessary to have a grasp of the basics of his theory.

Assimilation, Accommodation and Adaptation

Adaptation is a biological mode of functioning that characterizes all forms and levels of life. It consists of the dual processes of assimilation and accommodation, which go on continuously. Assimilation is the process of taking in from the environment all forms of stimulation and information, which are then organized and integrated into the organism's existing forms or structures. Accommodation implies modification of the structures of the organism so that it can adapt to the environment.

The young infant investigating his immediate environment, grasps, sucks, explores, probes and absorbs it, assimilating the experiences. But the environment, whether of inert objects or living things, resists, moves, rewards and punishes the infant, compelling him to accommodate, to adjust to new and changing conditions, so that pre-existing patterns of behaviour are modified to cope with new information or feed-back from the external situations.

Piaget states that intellectual growth is propelled by disequilibrium, by a failure of accommodative and assimilative processes to keep pace with one another, by failure of the child's models of the environment to suffice in coping with newly learned complexities of that environment, giving rise to the jest that it is the 'trouble theory of development.'

Assimilation, Accommodation - an example: If I present you with the following numbers: 2 and 4, and ask you to decide what the next number is, you will probably form the theory that this is a progression of even numbers and therefore that the next number in the series is 6. When I tell you that you are correct you assimilate this information into your theory. The information fits. I now ask you to provide the next number in the series and you will probably surmise that it is 8. However, this time I have to tell you that your answer is wrong and that the correct answer is 10. You are now in a state of disequilibrium, to use Piaget's terminology, and until you accommodate to the new information you will remain in disequilibrium. In order to attain a steady state or equilibrium you must re-organize your theory, in order to reach a balance between assimilation and accommodation. You can see why it is called the trouble theory of development. The progression is achieved by adding the last number to the penultimate number in the series, so the next will be 10 plus 6. We can summarize this cognitive process by saying:

> because of the intellect's organisation it exhibits adaptation, a two-way process comprising accommodation and assimilation.

Physical, Logico-mathematical and Social-arbitrary Knowledge

The concept of equilibration is a dynamic one, and it is therefore necessary to indicate what upsets the organism once it has achieved equilibrium. The first dynamic factor is maturation, the physiological growth of the genetic organic structures. Maturation only opens up future possibilities in Piaget's scheme, experience is also necessary to actualize the potential, experience derived from commerce with the environment. These interactions with the environment lead the child to construct two different kinds of knowledge: physical and logico-mathematical.

Physical knowledge is associated with the results of actions on objects: touching, lifting, throwing, hitting, smelling etc. To construct this knowledge the child must have repeated active experiences in which he carries out manipulations of objects. When constructing physical knowledge the physical properties of the objects themselves correct or reinforce the child's learning. Implicit in Piaget's conception of the development of the child is the idea that children acquire knowledge about the physical properties of objects by manipulating the objects and that all other ways of coming to know objects are qualitatively inferior. Reading about or listening to someone talk about an object cannot provide the quality of physical knowledge that can be acquired by active manipulation, a fact that is acknowledged by Gagné:

> The great value of concepts as means of thinking and communicating is the fact that they have concrete references.... but since concepts are learned by the human being via language, there is often the danger of losing sight of this concreteness. Learning can become over-verbalized which means that the concepts learned are highly inadequate in their reference to actual situations. The learner does not really know the meaning of the word even though he can use it correctly in a sentence. (Gagné, 1970, p.187)

Logico-mathematical knowledge is derived from acting upon objects, but does not come from the objects themselves, it is constructed from the child's actions on the objects. Logical relationships are constructed in the child's mind, such as higher, lower, faster. Mathematical relationships also are not implicit in objects but are constructed by the observing or counting child. Number and number-related concepts are logico-mathematical types of knowledge, but number is not a quality or characteristic of an object, it is an invention of each child.

Of course, physical knowledge and logico-mathematical knowledge develop in an inter-dependent manner, being tied together in their formation.

The third factor contributing to cognitive development is the transmission of social-arbitrary knowledge. Here information is learned from other children or transmitted by parents, teachers, or books in the process of education. Children learn language, values, rules, morality and symbol systems, in fact social-arbitrary knowledge is everything that is handed on from generation to generation, that which constitutes the essential foundation of human society. Piaget believes that when a child hears contradictory statements concerning this realm of knowledge his equilibrium is disturbed, effecting a search for an answer which will reduce the cognitive conflict.

It is the equilibration process which co-ordinates and regulates the three factors of cognitive development (maturation, experience and social-arbitrary knowledge), bringing about progressive states of equilibrium. Equilibration is the organizing factor underlying all biological and intellectual development.

The Relation between Subject and Object

An implicit assumption in behaviourist, stimulus-response psychology is that knowledge is a copy of reality. It is also a frequent assumption of traditional and conventional educational practice.

Piagetian thought provokes the question: is knowledge a copy of reality or is it a unique, individual construction? The traditional view has been that knowledge is a directly acquired copy of reality, the child was thought to incorporate accurate images of the real world directly. The latest ideas in cognitive psychology reject this idea. As Neisser (1967) puts it in his 'Cognitive Psychology':

> Whatever we know about reality has been mediated, not only by organs of sense but by complex systems which interpret and re-interpret sensory information. (Neisser, 1967, p.3)

Piaget's major contention is that each individual constructs reality, and for each child this is a unique construction: and this is what he means when, in 'The Science of Education and the Psychology of the Child', he says:

> Knowledge is derived from action, not in the sense of simple associative responses, but in a much deeper sense of assimilation of reality into the necessary and general co-ordination of action. To know an object is to act upon it and transform it.... intelligence consists in executing and co-ordinating actions, though in an interiorised and reflective form. (Piaget, 1971, p.28-29)

For Piaget, children's conceptions develop from those initially based on limited information - unrefined and frequently inaccurate schemes - to increasingly more accurate and refined schemes. The essential functions of intelligence consist in understanding and inventing, in other words of building up structures by structuring reality.

In relation to the different types of knowledge that may be acquired Piaget (1971) describes two aspects of thinking that are different but functionally related: the figurative aspect and the operative aspect.

Figurative Knowledge

The person looking at a tree sees it figuratively, but in his mind he also conceives it as alive, breathing, having roots, branches etc. These latter aspects are operative conceptions that go beyond the limitations of the former figurative knowledge. Figurative thoughts are perceptions, imitations, mental images, those aspects of thought that deal with states as they appear in the senses. They are the thoughts that occur at the time of perception of external objects, or at the perception of mental images. When we look at an object and our thought produces identification of that object - that is figurative thought.

A child looking at a tree sees leaves, branches etc: what she sees is figurative knowledge about the tree.

Operative Knowledge

Operative thought is the product of perceptions (figurative) and intelligence. Operative knowing is the product of transformations of states resulting from actions. It is the organization, consolidation and interaction of figurative knowledge, and intellectual development can be characterized as the growth of operative knowledge.

Operative and figurative knowing are related. Figurative knowledge feeds the development of operative knowledge - it is its source. And, of course, changes in operative knowing result in changes in our subsequent perceptions. Thus, the child looking at the tree who realizes that it is alive (operative knowledge) looks at it in a different way and no longer gets the same figurative knowledge.

The Theory of Stages

According to Piaget, the organization of intelligence changes qualitatively in several stages throughout the individual's life. Similar conceptual processes are thought to account for strategies employed at each stage.

Figure 6-1. Piagetian Stages of Cognitive Development.

		MENTAL AGE
I	SENSORIMOTOR PHASE	0-1.5 years
II	PRE-OPERATIONAL PHASE	1.5-7 years
	(i) Pre-conceptual stage	(1.5-4 years)
	(ii) Stage of intuitive thought	(4-7 years)
III	CONCRETE OPERATIONS PHASE	7-11 years
IV	FORMAL OPERATIONS PHASE	11 years and over

The order of the stages is fixed, each stage being regarded as essential preparation for the next one. In part, the stages are a result of maturation of the nervous system of the growing child. However, maturation is necessary but not sufficient for cognitive development: biological maturation does nothing more than open the way to possible constructions. It is interaction with the environment which actualizes them. Piaget acknowledges that some pedagogical interventions can accelerate and complete development (the American question according to Piaget) but they cannot change the order of constructions. There are also untimely pedagogical interventions such as teaching children to count before they have any concept of number.

Piaget (1970) identifies three principal periods of development: a) a sensorimotor period, which lasts until approximately 1.5 years of age; b) a period of representative intelligence which leads to concrete operations, running from 1.5-2 years to 11 years; c) finally, a period of propositional or formal operations, starting at about 11 years. There are, however, various sub-divisions, each of which is identified by particular cognitive characteristics (Figure 6-1).

Sensorimotor Phase

During the initial eighteen months of life the child begins by exercising its inborn reflexes and eventually co-ordinates its actions and perceptions to form acquired adaptations. In later life, in the school, the child will deal with his environment chiefly through his thoughts; the baby deals with it through its senses and motor activity. It is a period of pre-linguistic intelligence which allows, even without the use of language, certain rudimentary constructions, such as learning that objects are conserved and the development of notions of space and time. It is this period of child functioning that enables Piaget to place such emphasis on actions as the roots of logical operations.

> Turning to the question of the relations between language and logical operations, we have always maintained that the origin of logical operations is both deeper than and genetically prior to language; that is, it lies in the laws of the general co-ordinations of action, which control all activities including language itself. (Piaget, 1970, p.722)

Pre-operational Phase

This phase is divided into two stages. During the first, the pre-conceptual stage, the child represents one thing by another, plays games of pretence, plays some constructional games, draws and talks, learns letters and may read and write, but forms no true concepts and is considered to be egocentric. The child makes its first attempts at generalization at this stage, forming 'pre-concepts', which fall somewhere between mental images and true concepts (Pulaski, 1980). A pre-concept reveals the confusion between a class of objects and its members: one man is Daddy, so all men are daddies; one slug is much like the next, so the child will say 'There's the slug' on seeing one, and 'There's the slug again' on seeing another a few yards further on.

The second stage, the intuitive stage, starts at about four years. The child begins to form concepts but only sees one relationship in complex arrays and is dominated by perceptual judgements. The intuitive stage is so-called because it lacks the stable, reversible character of true operational thinking. It is typified by non-conservation in one of Piaget's most famous experiments. One of two glasses is partially filled with a liquid, and the second glass is then filled up to the same level. The child is asked if there is the same amount in both glasses, and adjustments are made until the child agrees that there is the same amount. The liquid from one of the glasses is now poured into another vessel, which is narrower and taller. To the question 'Is there more, less or the same amount?' in the tall, thin vessel, the child will reply that there is more, justifying the answer by focusing on a single dimension, even when the liquid is returned to the original glass.

During the pre-operational phase the child focuses his attention on the separate states or configurations of an array rather than on the transformations by which one state is transformed into another and such mental images as exist move slowly from one static configuration to the next, with no reversibility or flexibility, rather like slides in a projector. These are the figurative aspects of thought, in contrast to the operative aspects which are dynamic, related to transformations and external or internal actions.

Concrete Operations Phase

During the period from seven to eleven years physical actions are replaced by mental operations, the child forms classes and series but still works by trial and error, does not plan ahead and has difficulty with verbal definitions.

The child's mind at this stage is still tied to concrete experiences, even though hypotheses may be formed which go beyond the concrete evidence before them. Conservation, first of substance, followed by weight and then volume, is crucial to this stage. This requires an operational knowledge of reversal and involves the crucial process of decentring.

The child is capable of forming consistent classifications as concepts, rather than the pre-concepts formed by transductive reasoning in the previous stage. Related to classification is the ability to order similar objects according to size or position, a process known as seriation.

There are limitations in verbal reasoning, and when asked to use verbal propositions instead of objects, children at this stage tend to consider one statement at a time, just as children in the intuitive stage consider one relationship at a time when dealing with objects. The result is that concrete operational children have difficulty with such problems as: Edith is fairer than Susan; Edith is darker than Lily; who is the darkest of the three? They reason that Edith and Susan are fair, Edith and Lily are dark, therefore Lily is darkest, Susan is fairest, with Edith in between.

Related to the difficulties experienced with interiorized verbal reasoning is the difficulty in planning, especially in scientific experiments where the child tends to work by trial and error, rather than in a systematic manner.

Formal Operations Phase

The highest levels of thinking found in this phase are

only possible when the child can follow the form of an argument without having the concrete materials at hand. This is the stage at which children begin to reason hypothetically, in the absence of material evidence. Hypotheses can then be tested to determine real solutions amongst possible solutions, a process known as hypothetico-deductive reasoning.

There is no higher phase than formal operations, and this represents the peak of human cognitive development, the functioning of the mature organism. Although it may represent the final phase, it does not follow that all adults actually achieve the full potential of this phase, indeed, many adults may remain in the previous stage and fail to show those characteristics associated with formal operations: reasoning increasingly in verbal propositions, making hypotheses which they test, planning ahead, seeking to explain events, considering many possibilities and looking for general laws.

PIAGET AND EDUCATION

Active Methods

In 'The Science of Education and the Psychology of the Child', Piaget acknowledged that direct instruction and imposed labour are a necessary part of education _but_ he emphasized that educational programmes should 'give rise to active manipulation and discovery by the child itself.' Piaget is saying that basic operational structures of intelligence are not acquired through _instruction_ but must be invented by the child. Furthermore, the child must reach an appropriate stage of maturational and intellectual readiness before she will be able to develop new structures of thought. The goal for education, according to Piaget, is to produce individuals who are critical, creative and inventive discoverers. So a major part of the child's learning depends on experimentation and discovery.

Piaget states that an active school is not necessarily a school of manual labour and, although a child's activity at certain levels necessarily entails the manipulation of objects, at other levels the most authentic research activity may take place in the spheres of reflection requiring the most advanced forms of abstraction or verbal manipulations.

A criticism of such methods has been that they inevitably lead to anarchic individualism, but Piaget counters this by suggesting that far from this, they actually help to combine individual work and team work, and encourage self-discipline and voluntary effort.

At the time of writing 'The Science of Education and

Psychology of the Child' (1971) Piaget felt that although active methods were gradually becoming accepted, no great progress had been made because of the difficulty of putting them into practice when compared with receptive methods. Active methods require much more varied and concentrated work from the teacher, whereas giving lessons is less demanding and tiring, and corresponds to a much more natural tendency in the adult generally, and in the adult pedagogue in particular.

Also, an active pedagogy presupposes a much more advanced kind of training and without an adequate knowledge of child psychology the teacher cannot properly understand the students' spontaneous procedures and therefore fails to take advantage of reactions that to him seem quite insignificant and a mere waste of time. Piaget claims that 'the heart-breaking difficulty in pedagogy... is, in fact, that the best methods are also the most difficult ones' (1971, p.69).

The active classroom has been associated with the term progressive teaching, which has pupils in an active role, learning predominantly by discovery techniques, with an accent on creative expression. Subject matter tends to be integrated, with the teacher acting as a guide to educational experiences and encouraging co-operative work. External rewards and punishments are seen as being unnecessary, and there is not so much concern with traditional academic standards and testing.

Receptive Methods

Piaget compares active methods with receptive methods, which are also referred to as traditional methods of teaching, in which the child is the passive receiver of information transmitted by the teacher. The danger with such methods, according to Piaget, is that the resulting knowledge will frequently be rote learned and not fully understood. In other words, receptive teaching methods lead to a predominance of figurative knowledge rather than the higher goal of operative knowledge.

Receptive methods place greater emphasis on the creative role of the adult, with a consequent emphasis on the transmission of knowledge by the teacher, rather than the constructive role of action which leads to placing an essential share of importance upon the activities of the student.

The accent is on memory, practice and rote learning, with a concern for regular testing and competitive, academic standards. The pupils are essentially passive and there is little emphasis on their creative expression.

Intuitive or Audio-visual Methods

Periodically emphasis has been placed on the role of audio-visual methods, according to Piaget. He uses the term 'intuitive' for such teaching methods, equating the function of audio-visual aids with the 'intuitive stage' in his developmental scheme, a period before operative thought is established, and during which figurative aspects of knowledge predominate. He accuses well-intentioned pedagogues of using such aids and believing that they have reached the summit of educational progress when, in fact, they are multiplying intuitive figurations in forms that no longer have anything active in them.

Piaget quotes an experiment which illustrates the dangers of these 'intuitive figurations.' He compared the memories that groups of children retain of a grouping of cubes, according to whether the cubes had been:

1. simply looked at
2. reconstructed by the child itself
3. constructed by an adult while the child watched.

Piaget found that the direct experience is superior (Piaget, 1971, p.35), and the demonstration by an adult is no better than the simple observation of the completed grouping. Thus, Piaget concludes, by carrying out experiments in the child's presence, either as demonstrations or on film, instead of making him carry them out, one loses the entire informational and formative value offered by direct action.

Piaget goes on to suggest that an additional reason why active methods have not been taken up is the confusion that sometimes occurs between active and intuitive methods: that they are either equivalent or at least the intuitive methods produce all the benefits that can be derived from the active methods. This arises from two confusions:

1. that any activity on the part of the student or child is a matter of physical actions. This is only true at the elementary levels, not in the later stages when a student may be totally active in the sense of making a personal rediscovery of the truths to be acquired, even though his activity is being directed toward interior and abstract reflection
2. a belief that an activity dealing with concrete objects is no more than a figurative process, in other words nothing but a way of producing a sort of precise copy in perceptions or mental images of the objects in question.

In other words, some audio-visual theorists believe that a mechanical copy of an object or situation, as in a film or still picture, enables the child to gain knowledge of the object or situation. This is not so, as the experiment with the blocks revealed, knowledge is not at all the same thing as making a figurative copy of reality for oneself, it invariably consists of operative processes leading to a transformation of reality, ie. knowledge goes beyond the surface appearances.

Piaget is complaining about the rote-learning aspect of education, whereby the student makes a figurative mental copy of, for example, the stages of Piagetian theory, which are then duplicated in the examination or essay, without attempting to fit this information into previously acquired knowledge and experience in order to transform the old and new information in the process of thinking which leads ultimately to understanding.

Thus, intuitive methods merely provide students with speaking visual representation either of objects or events themselves or of the result of possible operations, but without leading to any effective realization of those operations. Piaget says that these methods are traditional methods which are continually reborn from their own ashes.

He concedes that they do certainly constitute an advance in relation to purely verbal or formal techniques, but they are totally inadequate in developing the child's operative activities and it is only as a result of a simple confusion between figurative and operative aspects of thought that it has been believed possible to pay tribute to the ideal of the active methods while at the same time giving concrete form to the subject matter of education in this purely figurative guise.

He relates this to the use of Cuisenaire rods, which are capable of being used in diametrically opposed ways:

1. a genuinely operative method, in which the child spontaneously manipulates the rods and forms configurations which lead to true operative understanding
2. intuitive or figurative methods, in which the teacher demonstrates and explains configurations laid out by the teacher rather than the child.

He also describes the use of a film to demonstrate geometrical concepts, including an illustration of Pythagoras's theorem in which the 'relations involved acquired visual clarity worthy of the highest praise.' But, Piaget asks 'Is this really training the child in geometrical reasoning and in operative construction in general?'

Pedagogy based on the image, even with the apparent dynamism of the film, remains inadequate for the training of operational constructivism, because intelligence cannot be reduced to a series of images on film. Piaget suggests that it might more correctly be compared to a series of cybernetic mechanisms ensuring a continuous flow of images by dint of auto-regulating and auto-correcting processes. This in turn leads to the conclusion that computer simulations with interaction between student and the machine may be more acceptable to Piaget.

Programmed Methods

Piaget's views of the figurative, rote-learning aspect of education are developed more fully in his criticisms of behaviouristic psychology, particularly as applied as an educational psychology. Piaget has this to say about behaviourism:

> This empty box conception of the organism, as it has been called, thus deliberately thumbs its nose at all kind of mental life, human or animal, and confines itself solely to behaviour in its most material aspects, ignoring any possible search for explanations in order to concentrate exclusively on the broad laws revealed by scrupulously detailed experimentation.
>
> This being so, Skinner, already in possession of the laws of learning he had personally verified or evolved, and freed of any theoretical preoccupations that might have hampered his testing of their general or practical application, observed in the first place that his experiments always worked much better when the interventions of the human experimenter were replaced by efficient mechanical apparatus. In other words, the pigeons produced much more regular reactions when dealing with teaching machines capable of applying the stimuli with greater precision and fewer minute variations. Skinner, a teacher by profession as well as a learning theorist, then had the brilliant idea that this observation of his would be equally valid when applied to humans, and that teaching machines, provided they were sufficiently well-programmed, would produce better results than an oral method of teaching susceptible of great variation in its application. And since the empty box conception of the organism renders so many preliminary considerations of the internal factors of human learning unnecessary, it was sufficient to be familiar with the general laws of learning and with the subject matter of the branches of knowledge to be taught, in order to construct programs at least equal in content to the body of knowledge commonly acquired.
>
> The experiment was tried and proved a total success. And it goes without saying, if we confine ourselves to

> the usual methods of teaching by means of verbal transmission and receptive processes, that it could not fail to succeed. (Piaget, 1971, p.76-77)

Piaget does have some good words for Skinner's machines because they 'provide evidence of good psychology in that they make use exclusively of positive reinforcement and dispense totally with negative sanctions or punishments.' Further, he is not saddened by the fact that school teachers can be replaced by machines because this demonstrates the mechanical nature of traditional teaching methods, which merely require the repetition of what has been transmitted. The machines may even demonstrate the failure of traditional methods to accomplish their rather limited aims.

Piaget also appreciates the greater intensity of motivation found with machines than that found in many traditional lessons and questions whether the teacher's affectivity always performs a desirable function. He is, in fact, much more positive about teaching machines than may be anticipated from some of his earlier remarks:

> In a time of great increase in student population and the scarcity of teachers they (teaching machines) are able to render undeniable services, and, in general, save a great deal of time in comparison with traditional methods of teaching. They are used not only in schools but also in commercial concerns where, for one reason or another, a necessity exists for rapid instruction of adults.
>
> Generally speaking, since every discipline must include a certain body of acquired facts as well as the possibility of giving rise to numerous research activities and activities of re-discovery, it is possible for a balance to be struck, varying from subject to subject, between the different parts to be played by memorizing and free activity. In which case, it is possible that the use of teaching machines will save time that would have been needlessly wasted by more traditional methods and therefore augment the number of hours available for active work. So that, particularly if the periods of active work include team work, with all that such work entails in the way of mutual incentives and checks, while the machine pre-supposes an essentially individualized kind of work, then this balance would at the same time be realizing yet another necessary kind of balance: that between the collective and individual aspects of intellectual effort, both so essential to harmonious school life. (Piaget, 1971, p.78-79)

Thus, according to Piaget, there is room for programmed

instruction, provided it is realized that it will be useful only in terms of acquiring facts (in a figurative manner). There must also be opportunities for activities and particularly manipulations which will lead to acts of discovery or re-discovery for the development of operational knowledge of a subject. But, such activities should not be misconstrued as being related to the use of audio-visual aids, which are perceptually dominated intuitive methods, producing figurative knowledge rather than true operational processes.

Research and Evaluation of Piagetian Theory

Piaget's contribution to cognitive psychology offers a considerable challenge to educational technology, because it personifies an alternative 'world-view' of educational matters. The emphasis is not on mechanical copies of reality as the basis of knowledge and understanding, but on active, or rather inter-active, processes of construction. Hence the choice of his 'cybernetic' analogy for intelligence in opposition to the mechanical film analogy. Piaget's view offers, in many ways, a richer framework for viewing cognition because it is based on a more complex model, which in turn has benefitted from richer conceptualizations and analogies than those available to the early behaviourists.

There have, however, been many criticisms of Piaget's theories and their educational applications, and it is necessary to take these into account before reaching a final evaluation of the potency of Piagetian ideas for educational technology.

It is necessary to point out that the age ranges given for the various stages are subject to substantial variation, predominant culture having a particularly strong effect. Shayer's (1978) investigation demonstrated the degree to which pupils in London comprehensives attained formal operations according to Piaget's time-scale. In fact, only 5.6% of 11 to 12-year-olds had reached the initial stages of formal operations, although many of the tasks demanded of students in the science classes were based on the assumption that a majority of pupils were in early formal operations, and could only be completed satisfactorily by the tiny minority of formal operational thinkers in this age range.

Clearly, the physical manipulation of objects and concrete experiences made available throughout the period of concrete operations, should also be available beyond the early years of secondary schooling and may even be required throughout the final years of schooling for many students.

There is some evidence to support the effects of manipulation rather than mere observation of manipulation by a teacher or instructor. For example, Macbeth (1974) found that the direct first-hand manipulative experiences in the development of process skills in elementary school science supported the theoretical literature that pre-operational children must operate on concrete objects, though such manipulations may be more important for younger rather than older elementary school children.

There is also some evidence in secondary school science provided by Gabel and Sherwood (1980). In this case students who manipulated molecular models made greater progress than those merely observing teacher manipulation of the models.

However, although there is some support for Piaget's emphasis on the need for manipulation and active involvement in learning, his ideas concerning heuristics or discovery learning have received little empirical support.

Certainly, advocates of discovery approaches, such as Shulman and Keislar (1966), have claimed that discovery motivates more effectively than receptive learning approaches, and Suchman (1961) claimed that:

> The need for improvement is great. Current educational practice tends to make children less autonomous and less empirical in their search for understanding as they move up the elementary grades. The schools must have a new pedagogy with a new set of goals which subordinate retention to thinking. (Suchman, 1961, p.151)

Whereas others, such as Skinner (1968), have pointed out that discovery learning is highly inefficient because it involves a relatively high degree of trial and error responding. Wittrock's review of research (1966) offers no conclusive evidence for assuming any advantage for discovery approaches. He suggests that as a way to learn a few specific associations, discovery learning may be inferior to more highly directed procedures, but with the learning of concepts and hierarchically ordered subject matter, discovery may fare better, as Gagné and Brown (1961) had found.

Brainerd (1977) in a sustained critique of Piagetian theory reviewed alternative learning approaches to the acquisition of conservation. According to Piaget teaching children concepts that have not spontaneously developed is completely useless, and he asks, is it good to accelerate the acquisition of these concepts anyway? Brainerd accuses Piaget of being transparently Rousseauian and suggests that Piaget's proposal 'all but trivializes learning research.' Further, he feels that Piaget's collaborators merely aim to confirm existing Piagetian laws, rather than the discovery of new ones and this makes it difficult to become enthusiastic about experiments 'whose horizons are so limited.' What Brainerd calls 'tutorial methods', which includes all familiar procedures from classical learning theory and social learning theory, were universally condemned by Sinclair (1973) and early evidence (Smedslund, 1961; Wohlwill and Lowe, 1962) certainly showed no evidence for learning effects on conservation tasks. However, other methods have been devised, including simple correction, rule learning, observational learning and conformity training, all of which yield positive results. Conformity training places a non-conserving child with a group who are conservers. The group is asked to observe a conservation experiment and to discuss each question and comment on the result, but they are restricted to formulating a consensual answer. Murray (1972) the originator of the technique found that 80% of pre-test non-conservers learned five conservation concepts and transfered these to two untrained conservation concepts. More recently Murray (1983) has commented on the fact that although shifts have generally been in the direction of conservation, there is no reason why the shift should not be in the other direction, according to social learning theory. However, although small numbers of conservers yield their position in the conformity situation, none revert to non-conservation on further tests, which means that there must be a powerful interactive effect between organismic maturation and the learning conditions.

There is no easy resolution of the two competing approaches because, as Murray (1983) concludes, 'each debater sees the child's deficiency or errors as due to a factor the other sees as tautological and non-falsifiable.'

On a different scale the Piagetian ideals of the active, discovery approach to teaching, have had a turbulent history when comparisons have been made with more traditional approaches. But, once again, there are different expectations associated with the two approaches. Lavatelli's 'Early Childhood Curriculum' (1970) concentrated on many concrete-operational concepts but did not show that a Piagetian programme produced a deeper understanding than any other system. Weikert (1973) found similar results, which were repeated in the purest of the Piagetian programs, the University of Wisconsin's 'Piagetian Preschool Education Programme' (Bingham-Newman, 1974).

Results from comparisons of approaches adopting many of the features associated with Piagetian methods have also been disappointing. Bennett (1976) ranged teacher styles along a twelve point continuum, from informal/progressive to formal/traditional, and identified a large group of teachers who closely matched the characteristics of the three major groupings: formal, mixed and informal. Data were collected for pupil performance at the start of the school year and then one year later on standard tests for reading, maths and English, together with measures for creative writing, punctuation and spelling, pupil behaviour and pupil personality.

The results indicated that pupils taught by formal and mixed styles show significantly superior progress as compared with those taught by informal styles, with the effect being more noticeable in average and above average achievers. In maths the formal style was superior to both mixed and informal, with the superiority existing at almost every level; and this result was confirmed in the English test.

The most difficult result for the progressive camp was not the fact that the more formal the teaching, the more time the students spent working on the subject matter at hand, hence the better the performance in reading, maths and English, but the fact that pupils in progressive settings did not perform at a higher level in their creative writing than their formally taught colleagues. Bruner (1976) who in much of his early writing had supported the discovery approach (Bruner, 1961) felt that the results indicated that 'common sense and technical inquiry are finally catching up with the romantic excess' and that 'new studies are now pointing to the critical role of the adult tutor, in social and intellectual development.' He did, however, urge caution in interpreting the results:

> The progressives' fallacy was the assumption that you arrive at the terminus immediately - self-directed from the start and not just later. Now we know better. Self-direction is wasteful if one does not know where one is going or why. But to swing back to a Prussian model of authoritarian teaching will only assure that the pendulum will keep going through its dull, historically repetitive trajectory. (Bruner, 1976, p.225)

In fact, Bennett's book encouraged a great deal of debate about the issue of progressive versus traditional teaching, and also about the actual techniques of data collection and analysis in such studies. Bennett undertook a re-analysis of the original data using more appropriate procedures (Aitken, Bennett and Hesketh, 1981) as did others (Gray and Satterly, 1981) and the results led to the conclusion that:

> First, the differences between teachers within styles were far greater than the differences between styles. Thus, one found 'effective' and 'ineffective' teachers, no matter which teaching style they adopted. Second, differences between teaching styles were so small as to be overwhelmed by differences between other systematic effects. And third, the direction of the differences between teaching styles did not consistently favour more 'formal' approaches over 'informal' ones. (Gray and Satterly, 1981, p.187)

These conclusions indicate that there is no easy answer to the progressive-traditional dilemma, certainly there seems to be no good evidence to support the superiority of traditional methods in reading, English and maths, and equally no more support for activities such as creative writing in the progressive classroom.

Aspects of this controversy are now emerging in the application of computers in education, in particular in the ideas of Seymour Papert and the ways in which the computer language LOGO should be used in the classroom.

PAPERT AND LOGO

Piagetian theory continues to exert an influence on teaching and the most recent form this has taken is the computer language LOGO developed by Seymour Papert, who describes in his book 'Mindstorms' (1980) the motivation which led to its creation:

> I take from Jean Piaget a model of children as builders of their own intellectual structures. Children seem innately gifted learners, acquiring long before they go to school a vast quantity of knowledge by a process I call Piagetian learning or learning without being taught. (Papert, 1980, p.7)

However, he does differ in some ways from Piaget, and takes maths as an example of a case where Piaget would explain the slower development of a particular concept by its greater complexity or formality; Papert sees the relative cultural impoverishment in those materials that would make the concept simple and concrete, as the major element. In the case of mathematics this leads to mathophobia! Papert argues that since it is easier to learn French in France, then it should be easier to learn maths in mathsland. LOGO has been developed to provide a mathsland where children encounter and solve fundamental mathematical problems while achieving simple goals like drawing a house or snail.

Papert observes that children learn to speak naturally and easily, but they do not acquire equal competence in mathematical activities. He suggests that the difference lies not in innate differences nor even in the amount of learning, but in the nature of the learning process itself: it consists of learning the manipulation of symbols in a manner alien to the child's experience, using an unsuitable technology (paper and pencil). With the right dynamic technology children can become real mathematicians, and the right technology is a computer with LOGO programming language. The computer can provide an interactive relationship, giving immediate feedback when errors occur, leading to meaningful learning of concepts in maths and other areas.

The method advocated by Papert is based on Piaget's learning by self-discovery, LOGO is a 'tool to think with' and the natural processes of learning should not be upset by teachers taking control. He argues (Papert, 1972) that the skills acquired during the design and debugging of programmes will be generalized, eventually being used to design and debug conceptual representations of problems. Papert feels that LOGO is capable of inducing general problem-solving strategies, rather than the 'domain-specific strategies induced from examples given by the teacher' (Howe, O'Shea and Plane, 1980).

There are many different ways in which any particular medium can be used in teaching, as Piaget (1971) noted, and LOGO is no exception. The Piagetian approaches adopted by Papert are 'horticulturalist' (Brainerd, 1978), with an emphasis on total intellectual growth derived from discovery learning, rather than traditional receptive methods which can only produce specific skills. Howe and his colleagues (Howe, O'Shea and Plane, 1980) adopt a more structured approach towards the use of LOGO. Howe (1979) has described his method as learning by model building, a process which enables students to learn about the underlying structure of an entity by building a model of it. Real learning is accomplished when the modeller can define a set of general principles which model a variety of entities. The structured approach developed by Howe is based on the following guidelines:

1. The teacher should always try to build on the child's existing knowledge.
2. The use of familiar materials (toys, pictures, apparatus) as manipulable models or metaphors makes teaching and learning more manageable.
3. Classroom teaching ought to be a partnership between teacher and child, with the child being given as much responsibility as possible for choosing, formulating and solving problems within the broad aims or objectives laid down by the teacher, in contrast to the very formal, rigid control used by many teachers.
4. Feedback of information to the learner is crucial, to check what has been done and to suggest what should be done in the event of failure.

There are many conflicting reports concerning the successes or failures of LOGO, and this arises from the different approaches to the nature of evaluation. Many studies have adopted an observational or case-study approach, following the pattern set by Piaget's method for obtaining data. Papert advocates taking a small group of pupils and working with them exclusively for the time required to test the new method, even in the face of protests from headmasters, teachers and school authorities. He claims that such a method would yield results so qualitatively different that the question 'How do you measure that?' would be meaningless, or the results would be so poor that it would be unnecessary to even ask the question. The Edinburgh group (Howe, O'Shea and Plane, 1980) disagree and have adopted a more formal assessment procedure, for as they say:

> .... we cannot ignore cost considerations, nor objections by educational authorities. In our experience, the most important constraint is the examination diet. (Howe, O'Shea and Plane, 1980, p.5)

Most of the research has concentrated on problem solving and the learning of mathematical skills, but in general results have been disappointing. Michayluk (1986) concludes that, methodology aside, there is little evidence of LOGO influencing such skills. In 1969, Feurzig taught algebra and arithmetic to 13-year-olds using LOGO, but with no overall improvement in their mathematics and Howe, O'Shea and Plane (1980) reported similar findings with bottom stream 11 to 12 year-olds, although they did find that the children became more self-confident and keener to discuss mathematics with teachers.

For many groups the lack of traditional experimental research data does not appear to cause any concern, their descriptive data leads them to the conclusion that LOGO does improve pupils' reasoning and problem-solving, and that the powerful ideas do generalize and transfer (Noss, 1983 and 1984; Hoyles, Sutherland and Evans, 1985). Hoyles and Sutherland's research indicates that LOGO can act as a catalyst for change in the classroom, but do caution that LOGO alone cannot make a poor learning situation into a good one: good organization is crucial. They conclude that LOGO is a powerful new tool for provoking reflection in pupils and that pupils learn to make use of the feedback that the computer provides. The emphasis is on the pupils having freedom to test out their conjectures and to develop their own styles of learning.

However, these are still early days for LOGO research, and it will be many years before a full appraisal will be possible.

Constructivism and Educational Technology

Structured or unstructured, there is a qualitative difference in the approach adopted by both practitioners when compared with behaviouristic methods. The purpose of education is the development of operative mental structures, rather than mere figurative, rote repetition, with children having much greater control over their learning activities. Educational technology must respond to the challenge of investigating these methods and the role such structures play in the development of the creative, innovative aspects of intelligence.

Behaviouristic and neo-behaviouristic methods may establish optimum learning of what is already known, but it is other methods, such as those advocated by Piaget and Papert, which may ultimately lead to the qualitatively different aspects of cognition associated with the invention of the presently unknown. Following the launching of the first man-made satellite by the U.S.S.R., on 4th October 1957, it was for just these reasons that Jerome Bruner's 'The Process of Education' (1960) became a best-seller in the early 1960's, in the U.S.

REFERENCES

Aitken, M.A., Bennett, S.N. and Hesketh, J. (1981) 'Teaching styles and pupil progress: a re-analysis', British Journal of Educational Psychology, 51, 170-186.

Bennett, S.N. (1976) Teaching Styles and Pupil Progress. London: Open Books.

Bingham-Newman, A.M. (1974) 'Development of Logical Abilities in Early Childhood. A Longitudinal Comparison of the Effects of Two Pre-school Settings.' Unpublished Doctoral Dissertation. University of Wisconsin, Madison. U.S.A.

Brainerd, C.J. (1977) 'Learning research and Piagetian theory'. In L. Seigal and C.J. Brainerd (Eds) Alternatives to Piaget: Critical Essays on the Theory.

Brainerd, C.J. (1978) Piaget's Theory of Intelligence. Englewood Cliffs, NJ.: Prentice-Hall.

Broadbent, D.E. (1958) Perception and Communication. Oxford: Pergamon Press.

Bruner, J.S. (1960) The Process of Education. Cambridge Mass.: Harvard University Press.

Bruner, J.S. (1961) 'The act of discovery', Harvard Educational Review, 31(1), 21-32.

Bruner, J.S. (1966) 'Some elements of discovery'. In L.S. Shulman & E.R. Keislar (Eds) Learning by Discovery. Chicago: Rand McNally.

Bruner, J.S. (1976) 'The styles of teaching', New Society, 29th April, 223-225.

Eysenck, M.W. (1984) A Handbook of Cognitive Psychology. London: Erlbaum.

Feurzig, W., Papert, S., Bloom, M., Grant, R. and Solomon, C. (1969) Programming Languages as a Conceptual Frame work for Teaching Mathematics. Mathematics, Report 1889, Cambridge, Mass.: Bolt Beranek and Newman.

Gabel, D. and Sherwood, R. (1980) 'The effect of student manipulation of molecular models on chemistry achievement according to Piagetian level', Journal of Research in Science Teaching, 17(1), 75-81.

Gagné, R.M. (1970) The Conditions of Learning (2nd. Edition). London: Holt, Rinehart and Winston.

Gagné, R.M. and Brown, L.T. (1961) 'Some factors in the programming of conceptual learning', Journal of Experimental Psychology, 62, 313-321.

Gray, J. and Satterly, D. (1981) 'Formal or informal? A re-assessment of the evidence', British Journal of Educational Psychology, 51, 187-196.

Howe, J.A.M. (1979) 'Learning through model-building.' In D. Mitchie (Ed) Expert Systems in the Micro-electronic Age. Edinburgh: Edinburgh University Press.

Howe, J.A.M., O'Shea, T. and Plane, F. (1980) Teaching Mathematics Through LOGO Programming: An Evaluation Study. DAI Research Paper No. 115, Edinburgh University.

Hoyles, C., Sutherland, R. and Evans, J. (1985) A Preliminary Investigation of the Pupil-centred Approach to the Learning of Logo in the Secondary School Mathematics Classroom. London: University of London Institute of Education.

Jonassen, D.H. (1985) 'Learning strategies: a new educational technology', Programmed Learning And Educational Technology, 22(1), 26-34.

Lavatelli, C. (1970) Early Childhood Curriculum - a Piaget Programme. Boston: American Science and Engineering.

Macbeth, D.R. (1974) 'The extent to which pupils manipulate materials and attainment of process skills in elementary school science', Journal of Research in Science Teaching, 11(1), 45-51.

Michayluk, J.O. (1986) 'LOGO: more than a decade later', British Journal of Educational Technology, 17(1), 35-41.

Murray, F.B. (1972) 'The acquisition of conservation through social interaction', Developmental Psychology, 6, 1-6.

Murray, F.B. (1983) 'Learning and development through social interaction and conflict: a challenge to social learning theory.' In L.S. Liben (Ed) Piaget and the Foundations of Knowledge. New Jersey: Lawrence Erlbaum.

Neisser, U. (1967) Cognitive Science. New York: Appleton-Century- Crofts.

Neisser, U. (1976) Cognition and Reality. San Francisco: Freeman.

Noss, R. (1983) Starting Logo: Interim Report of the Chiltern MEP Logo Project. Hatfield: MEP.

Noss, R. (1984) Children Learning Logo Programming: Interim

Report No.2. Hatfield: MEP.

Papert, S. (1972) 'Teaching children thinking', Programmed Learning and Educational Technology, 9, 245-255.

Papert, S. (1980) Mindstorms. Brighton: The Harvester Press.

Piaget, J. (1970) 'Piaget's theory'. In P.H. Mussen (Ed) Manual of Child Psychology, vol.1, 3rd Edition. London: John Wiley.

Piaget, J. (1971a) The Science of Education and the Psychology of the Child. London: Longmans.

Piaget, J. (1971) Biology and Knowledge. Chicago: Chicago University Press.

Pulaski, M. A. (1980) Understanding Piaget. London: Harper and Row

Shayer, M. (1978) 'The analysis of science curricula for Piagetian level of demand', Studies in Science Education, 5, 115-130.

Shulman, L.S. and Keislar, E.R. (1966) Learning by Discovery: A Critical Appraisal. Chicago: Rand-McNally

Sinclair, H. (1973) 'Recent Piagetian research in learning studies.' In M. Schwebel and J. Raph (Eds) Piaget in the Classroom. New York: Basic Books.

Skinner, B.F. (1968) The Technology of Teaching. London: Appleton-Century-Croft.

Smedslund, J. (1961) 'The acquisition of conservation of substance and weight in children. II. External reinforcement of conservation of weight and the operations of addition and subtraction', Scandanavian Journal of Psychology, 2, 71-84.

Suchman, J.R. (1961) 'Inquiry training: building skills for autonomous discovery', Merrill-Palmer Quarterly Behaviour and Development, 7, 147-169.

Waddington, C.H. (1957) The Strategy of the Genes. London: Allen and Unwin.

Weikert, D.P. (1973) Development of Effective Pre-school Programs: A Report on the High/Scope- Ypsilanti Pre-school Projects. Paper presented at the High/Scope Educational Research Foundation Conference, Ann Arbour, Michigan, USA.

Wittrock, M.C. (1966) 'The learning by discovery hypothesis.' In L.S. Shulman and E.R. Keislar (Eds) Learning by Discovery: A Critical Appraisal. Chicago: Rand-McNally.

Wohlwill, J.F. and Lowe, R.C. (1962) 'An experimental analysis of the conservation of number', Child Development, 33, 153-167.

CHAPTER 7

THOUGHT, CULTURE AND COGNITIVE MODELS

Piaget's theory has recently been criticized by Wartofsky (1983) for failing to adapt to new information and ideas in the field of cognitive development: there has been too much assimilation and not enough accommodation. This amounts to a criticism that the theory is no longer capable of growth. Wartofsky calls for a historical epistemology, rather than a genetic epistemology, because phylogenesis, in cognitive terms, can no longer be seen to be biologically fixed. It is historical, cultural and it continues. From this it follows that ontogenesis is not the socialization of child-thought to a fixed adult world, but to a changing world. Thus, Piaget cannot determine those universal and necessary features of the growth of knowledge, because this assumes a fixed species as the norm. What is needed, according to Wartofsky, is an evolutionary theory of the history of cognition. Implicit in this is the need for Piagetian theory to accommodate to new ideas and theories in order to develop and progress, and there is an implied criticism that this has not occurred.

Piagetian theory exerted a great influence on the early work of the American cognitive psychologist Jerome S. Bruner, following his visit to Geneva in 1956. However, Bruner has shown himself to be more receptive than his mentor to new ideas which have been in conflict with Piagetian theory. He has continued to admit his mistaken assumptions (Bruner, 1983) and press on with an evolving view of human development. Central to this is his use of the Lamarkian metaphor:

> Assume, for example, that man continues to adjust when he learns a language and certain ways of using tools. At that particular point evolution becomes Lamarkian in the sense of involving the passing on of acquired characteristics, not through the genes, but through the medium of culture. (Bruner, 1966a, p.101)

For Bruner culture is essential for humankind because it is a means of transmitting the accumulated knowledge of earlier generations. Each generation does not have to re-discover the past. It does, however, bring with it a certain vulnerability, in that it is reversible and may be forgotten as has happened in the Easter Islands and the Inca civilization of Peru.

Bruner's increasing emphasis on cultural aspects of

cognition, and in particular the amplification of cognition afforded by language, began with his contact with the works of the Soviet psychologist Vygotsky, who viewed intelligence as the capacity to benefit from instruction, with language having a powerful developmental role.

However, Bruner is still probably best known for his summary of the Woods Hole conference convened in 1959 by the National Academy of Sciences. Thirty-five 'scientists, scholars and educators' discussed ways in which education in science could be improved in primary and secondary schools, and the report of their deliberations was 'The Process of Education.'

The Process of Education

Paul Goodman announced in the N.Y. Herald Tribune that 'The Process of Education' (1960) was a classic comparable in its philosophical centrality and humane concreteness to Dewey's essays on education.

Bruner set forth a strong argument favouring the idea of models in the head based on general understanding, from which hypotheses about the particular could be generated and then tested against experience. According to Bruner the great disciplines (maths, physics, history) are not so much repositories of knowledge, they are methods for the use of mind. They provide the structure that gives meaning to the particulars, and the object of education is to get as swiftly as possible to that structure - to penetrate a subject, not to cover it. This is done by spiraling into it: a first pass to get the intuitive sense of it, later passes over the same domain to go more deeply into it.

Bruner complained that relatively little work by American psychologists had been done on the manner in which students could be trained to grasp the underlying structure of complex knowledge. He mentioned the latest researches which demonstrated that 'massive general transfer can be achieved by appropriate learning.' These studies were concerned with learning designed to produce general understanding of the structure of a subject, and as an example he considers mathematics:

> .... algebra is a way of arranging knowns and unknowns in equations so that the unknonwns are made knowable. The three fundamentals involved in working with these equations are commutation, distribution, and association. Once a student grasps the ideas embodied by these three fundamentals, he is in a position to recognize wherein 'new' equations to be solved are not

> new at all, but variants on a familiar theme. (Bruner, 1960, p.7)

This reflected the emphasis from the cognitive revolution of the 1950's concerning the generativeness of knowledge: knowledge is not a store-house. Learning is most often figuring out how to use what is already known in order to go beyond what is currently being thought - and this involves knowing something structural about what is being contemplated - how it is put together. As Bruner says 'Knowing how something is put together is worth a 1,000 facts about it. It permits you to go beyond it.' (Bruner, 1983, p.183)

Perhaps the most controversial statement in the book was that any subject can be taught to anybody at any age in some form that is honest. Bruner has since complained that this is easy to take too literally; he was simply arguing that there are many intuitive notions in a range of subjects (calculus, the theory of evolution etc.) whose early grasp would help learning of the later, fully developed idea.

This hypothesis was based on three general ideas. From Piaget he took the idea that the child's understanding of any mathematical, scientific or moral idea would be framed by the level of intellectual operations that he had achieved. Lower levels of understanding are routes to higher-level ones. The lower level is not a degraded version of the higher one - each has a logic of its own.

In addition to the Piagetian perspective Bruner suggested that the act of learning appeared to consist of three simultaneous processes: acquisition of new information; transformation of information to make it fit new tasks; and evaluation or checking whether the manipulated information is adequate to the task.

Finally, there was the idea of the 'spiral curriculum'. A curriculum ought to be built around the great issues, principles, and values that a society sees as worthy of continual relevance for its members, according to Bruner, and he demonstrates how this may be applied to science:

> So too in science. If understanding of number, measure and probability is judged crucial in the pursuit of science, then instruction in these subjects should begin as intellectually honestly and as early as possible in a manner consistent with the child's forms of thought. Let the topics be developed and redeveloped in later grades. Thus, if most children are to take a tenth-grade unit in biology, need they approach the subject cold? Is it not possible, with a minimum of formal laboratory work if necessary, to introduce them to some of the major biological ideas earlier, in a spirit perhaps less exact and more intuitive. (Bruner, 1960, p.54)

These ideas reflected the intellectual ferment of the times, particularly the structuralist influences of Chomsky, Levi-Strauss and Piaget, and there were many different reactions to such ideas. In Russia the book tripped off a debate on the dogmatism of Russian education; in Italy it was used to attack the decaying formalism of the right and the utilitarian pragmatism of the left. In Japan it caught a wave of reform and became an emblem against traditional learning by rote.

Modes of Representation

Following on from the success of 'The Process of Education' Bruner became concerned with the techniques and technologies that aid growing human beings to represent in a manageable way the recurrent features of the complex world in which they live. He noted that the principal change in man during the past half-million years has been by linking himself with new external implementation systems rather than by any conspicuous change in morphology - 'evolution by prosthesis' as the anthropologist Weston La Barre put it. Bruner quoted Washburn and Howell (1960) as evidence for this:

> It would appear that the large size of the brain of certain hominids was a relatively late development and that the brain evolved due to new selection pressures after bipedalism and consequent upon the use of tools.... (the) size of brain has increased some three-fold subsequent to the use and manufacture of implements. (Washburne and Howell, 1960, p.49)

Bruner suggested that the 'implement' systems have been of three main kinds:

1) Amplifiers of human motor capacities (levers, wheels, cutting tools).

2) Amplifiers of human sensory capacities (primitive devices such as smoke signals and modern ones such as radar).

3) Amplifiers of human ratiocinative (logical thought) capacities (language systems, explanatory theories).

He stated that these are conventionalized and transmitted by the culture, particularly the ratiocinative amplifiers, which involve symbol systems governed by rules that must be shared. He also suggested that there are three systems for processing information allowing human beings to construct what he calls 'models' of their worlds, which emerge in the developing child in the following order:

1) through action
2) through imagery
3) through symbols and language

These three modes of internal representation are termed:

1) through action........................ENACTIVE
2) through imagery.......................ICONIC
3) through symbols and language..........SYMBOLIC

Initially, Bruner saw the enactive phase running from very early in life, with language being superimposed at around 18 months and imagery declining at the age of 6 or 7 years: first comes enactive, then iconic and finally symbolic forms of representation. Bruner acknowledges in his autobiography 'In Search Of Mind' (1983) that he fell into the Genevan trap of postulating a chronological straight jacket. He now feels that these modes are present throughout life and are partially translatable into one another.

Enactive Mode:

The enactive mode of representation is highly manipulative in character. It is knowing some aspect of reality without the use of imagery or words. Hence, it consists of representing past events through making appropriate motor responses. It consists mainly of knowing how to do something; it consists of a series of actions that are appropriate for achieving some result eg. sailing a boat, tying a knot, riding a bike.

Iconic Mode:

This is based on internal imagery. The knowledge is represented by a set of images that stand for the concept. Iconic representation depends upon visual or other sensory organisation and is principally defined by perceptual organisation and techniques for economically transforming perceptions. Although initially seen as fading from use in the child's cognitive apparatus at the age of 6 or 7 years, it is now recognized as an important element in the highest intellectual realms. Consider what Einstein had to say about his thought processes:

> The words or language, as they are written or spoken, do not seem to play any role in my mechanisms of thought. The psychical entities which seem to serve as elements in thought are certain signs and more or less clear

> images which can be voluntarily reproduced or combined.... The above mentioned elements are, in my case, of visual and some of muscular type. Conventional words or other signs have to be sought for laboriously only in some secondary stage... (J. Hadamard, 1945)

We have a similar account of Kekule's discovery of the benzene ring in a dream:

> Again atoms were gamboling before my eyes. Smaller groups kept to the background. My mind's eye trained by repeated visions of a similar kind, now distinguished larger formations of various shapes.... everything in movement winding and turning like snakes. And look, what was that? One snake grabbed its own tail, and mockingly the shape whirled before my eyes. As if struck by lightning I awoke. (Anschutz, R., 1961, p.700)

And there are other examples, such as Watson and Crick's discovery of the DNA helix (J.D. Watson, 1968). Bruner is suggesting that images stand for perceptual events in the same way that a picture stands for the object pictured. In many circumstances such a representation of the world has many advantages, but, as we shall see, there are also disadvantages associated with predominantly iconic forms of representation.

Symbolic Mode:

Increasingly throughout life there is recourse to the symbolic mode of representation of thought. The emphasis here is that representation is based upon an abstract, arbitrary and flexible system of thought. It enables individuals to deal with what might be and what might not, and is a major tool in reflective thinking, though as we have seen not the only one. This mode is representative of a person's ability to consider propositions rather than objects (as we have seen in the stage of formal operations), to give concepts a hierarchical structure and to consider alternative possibilities in a combinatorial fashion.

Bruner gives the following example to distinguish between the three modes and to show how there is a natural progression from enactive through iconic to symbolic modes of thought:

> Any domain of knowledge (or any problem within that domain of knowledge) can be represented in three ways: by a set of actions appropriate for achieving a certain result (enactive representation); by a set of summary images or graphics that stand for a concept without defining it fully (iconic representation); and

> by a set of symbolic or logical propositions drawn from a symbolic system that is governed by rules or laws forming and transforming propositions (symbolic representation). The distinction can most conveniently be made concretely in terms of a balance beam.... A quite young child can plainly act on the 'principles' of a balance beam, and indicates that he can do so by being able to handle himself on a see-saw. He knows that to get his side down farther he has to move out farther from the centre. A somewhat older child can represent the balance beam to himself either by a model on which rings can be hung and balanced or by a drawing. The image of the balance beam can be varyingly refined, with fewer and fewer irrelevant details present, as in the typical diagrams in an introductory textbook in physics. Finally, a balance beam can be described in ordinary English, without diagrammatic aids, or it can be even better described mathematically by reference to Newton's Law of Moments in inertial physics. (Bruner, 1966b, p.45)

Dale (1969) found in Bruner's ideas a conceptual framework which related to the three main divisions of his 'Cone of Experience' in the fifth edition of 'Audio-visual Methods in Teaching.' He suggested that our experiences vary according to the degree in which they involve us physically or in thought. Some experiences call for a good deal of concrete, direct, immediate action in which we make full use of our senses and often our muscles as well. Observing something, however, requires less physical, or concrete, action than an experience of doing. And symbolic experiences have virtually all the manifest physical action removed. Dale agreed with Bruner that we begin our learning of a specific matter with a broad base of direct experience in action and gradually we omit these specific, first-hand, concrete occurrences and impressions as we come to rely on iconic substitutes or pictorial representations. At both stages, we develop a summarizing idea or symbol and when we understand a symbol we can use a word or formula to stand for everything out of which it developed.

> This visual analogy (the Cone of Experience) is one of several devices that have been set up to show the progression of learning experiences from direct, first-hand participation to pictorial representation and on to purely abstract, symbolic expression.... the threefold arrangement of learning possibilities illustrates the three kinds of experience that we have found so important in the process of complete communication. In this respect it is similar to the analysis of the three major modes of learning made by Jerome Bruner. (Dale, 1969, p.108)

Thought, Language and the Zone of Proximal Development

Bruner went on to develop his curriculum package 'Man: A Course Of Study', which was concerned with the nature of man as a species, and the forces that shape his humanity. Five great humanizing forces, each closely associated with man's evolution as a species, were explored (Bruner, 1966b). These were tool making, language, social organization, the management of man's prolonged childhood and man's urge to explain his world and they reflected Bruner's increasing interest in Vygotsky's functionalist psychology.

Vygotsky was a Russian Jew, deeply interested in the arts and in language, and was a friend of the film-maker Eisenstein. His objective was to explore how human society provided instruments to aid the developing individual mind, and how the child clumsily takes over the forms and tools of the culture and then learns to use them appropriately. His functionalist psychology was interested in studying how the child uses hints and takes advantage of others helping him organize his thought processes until he can do so on his own. Vygotsky (1962) used the term 'Zone of Proximal Development' to describe the child's potential to use the help of others to gain consciousness and reach higher ground intellectually, transforming the meaning of the lower order concepts. Intelligence tests were inadequate measures of a child's ability, as far as Vygotsky was concerned, because they only show what she is capable of on her own. In the real world children have access to older children and adults to help them solve their problems, and so he argued that we should take into account the capacity of a child to profit from help that others can give when assessing a child's potential. The more they take advantage of an adult's support, the wider is their 'Zone of Proximal Development.' Two children may both be at the same stage when measured by conventional tests but may differ in the extent of their respective zones. With help one may manage to complete tasks usually completed independently by children four years her senior, whereas the other with similar help may only manage to extend his competence by two years, the limit of his zone. Of course, Vygotsky was writing at a time when advanced technological aids,in the form of calculators and computers, were not available to children, but there is no reason why the concept of a zone of proximal development should not be extended to include help derived from such powerful aids.

Vygotsky, working with Luria in the 1920's and early 1930's, offered a challenge to the prevailing Soviet view of psychology, which was predominantly a Pavlovian atomistic view, based on the reflex. They placed much greater emphasis on the transforming power of language and the internalized linguistic system represented in thought. Vygotsky's genius was to exploit the distinction between classical conditioning prior to the growth of symbolic function, and thought after the intrusion of what Pavlov reluctantly termed the 'second signal system.'

He suggested that symbol systems restructure mental activity, and as symbol systems emerge in the course of history so different cognitions will be produced. Basic psychological processes (abstraction, generalization, inference) are universal and common to all humankind, but their functional organization will vary depending on the nature of the symbol systems available in different epochs. Language is a universal symbol system playing a crucial role in the development of higher psychological processes. Other symbol systems which are not universal introduce culture-specific differences. Luria (1976) led an expedition in the 1930's to test Vygotsky's theory and found that there were consitent differences between traditional non-literate farmers and other members of the same villages who had undergone brief literacy programmes. The most traditional and isolated populations with neither literacy nor schooling were context-bound, guided by perceptual and functional attributes and responded in a concrete manner to the tests. The most schooled group were able to respond in a more abstract manner and were more responsive to the conceptual and logical relationships between things. This certainly pointed to confirmation of Vygotsky's thesis that socio-cultural changes form the basis for the development of higher psychological processes, and literacy could be used as an indicator of the level of functioning. However, there were many comensurate changes at that time within Soviet society and differences in mental operations could not be attributed to literacy or schooling per se (Scribner and Cole, 1981).

This line of research has been pursued by Greenfield and Bruner (1966) who found similar results with Wolof children in Senegal. Greenfield has suggested that the differences are due to the school children's capacity for context-independent, abstract thought, and has provided a link between this and written language. Olson (1976) has also supported the theory that literacy biases cultures toward the development of formal reasoning systems. Scribner and Cole (1981) disagree having found no evidence to support the construct of a general 'literacy' phenomena. They suggest that literacies are highly differentiated and that the Arabic and Vai scripts studied did not trade off for each other in predicting cognitive performance, nor do they (singly or in combination) substitute for English literacy. Their results suggest a more general effect of the de-contextualization prevalent in the culture of Western schooling, as proposed by Donaldson (1978).

Cognition and Culture

Piaget always resisted the idea that there is a psychological reality to culture, that exists in the Popperian World 3 sense such that it can be internalized and serve as a prosthesis for the mind and development (Bruner, 1983), but for Bruner it became a crucial element in the child's development.

Bruner sees a person's maturing cognitive growth as being characterized by the increasing independence of his responses from the immediate nature of the stimuli and this growth depends upon the person internalizing events into a storage system that corresponds to aspects of the environment, by means of images, words, symbols. Through growth a person gains freedom from stimulus-control through mediating processes that transform the stimulus prior to the response.

Although Bruner sees mental growth as being like a staircase with rather sharp risers - a matter of spurts and rests, the spurts being touched off when capacities begin to develop, he differs from Piaget in that he believes that the steps or spurts are not very clearly linked to age; some environments can slow the sequence down or bring it to a halt, others move it along faster.

For example, Bruner anticipates improvement in performance in Piaget's conservation task when the environment is changed, forcing the child to activate language and take advantage of the 'remoteness of reference' that is a feature of language. In such a situation the child is forced to say his description of the world in the absence of the things to be described.

This was confirmed in Franks' perceptual shield experiment, reported in 'Studies in Cognitive Growth' (Bruner et al., 1966). Children who were not 'conservers' were shown two beakers of different dimensions, one containing liquid. A screen was placed in front of the beakers and the liquid poured from one to the other. The child was then asked 'Is there still the same amount of liquid?' In the traditional Piagetian conservation experiment children observe the pouring of the liquid from one beaker to the other and when asked if there is still the same amount of liquid they focus on the changed appearance and indicate that there is more or less depending on the dimensions of the beaker. Franks found that many children who failed on the traditional test were able to answer correctly with the shield in place. Correct responses jumped from 0% to 40% for the 4 year-old group, from 20% to 90% for 5 year-olds, and from 50% to 100% for 6 year-olds. The most common responses being 'its the same water' or 'you only poured it!' When the screen was removed all the 4-year-olds change their minds, the perceptual display overwhelmed them, but virtually all the 5-year-olds held to their judgements, often invoking the difference between appearance and reality in their defence: 'It looks like more to drink, but it is only the same because it is the same water and it was only poured from there to there.' All 6 and 7-year-olds also held to their judgement.

When a post-test was administered with a different set of test materials to those used in the experiment it was found that in most cases the change in the child's reasoning had generalized and it was concluded that it was attributable to the powerful organizing effects of language.

The experiment reflects Bruner's view that language is a powerful ratiocinative technology which provides the child with a qualitatively different model of the world to that based purely on observation and this enables the child to predict the outcome of manipulations of the environment more accurately. Such technological advances, in a cognitive sense, promote the development of intellectual functioning, according to Bruner:

> I shall take the view in what follows that the development of human intellectual functioning from infancy to such perfection as it may reach is shaped by a series of technological advances in the use of mind. Growth depends upon the mastery of techniques and cannot be understood without reference to such mastery. These techniques.... are skills transmitted with varying efficiency and success by the culture, language being a prime example. (Bruner, 1964, p.1)

Direct and Mediated Experience

Bruner's continuing interest in the interaction between cognition and the technologies of culture led him to consider the nature of experiences which are transformed and contribute to a person's internal model of the world.

He dealt with the various forms of direct and mediated experience in the 73rd Year Book of the National Society for the Study of Education under the title 'Learning Through Experience and Learning Through Media' (Olson and Bruner, 1974). These major aspects of learning, including the three modes of internal representation, are considered in terms of their partial equivalence and substitutability, and also their differing potential roles in the intellectual development and acculturation of children.

When discussing direct experience he suggests that organisms have commerce with the environment on their own terms and actively select those features which are necessary for the construction of representations of the environment which enable survival of the individual or species. From this it follows that 'our conception of physical reality is itself achieved by selective mediation' and it is the activities engaged in which determine the nature of such models of reality, as was suggested by Piaget (1971, Biology and Knowledge). Thus, we have a picture of reality that is biased or coded in terms of our actions upon it. Knowledge is always mediated or specified through some form of human activity and, according to Bruner and Olson, this activity has two facets:

1) Information about the world (knowledge)
2) Information about the activity used in gaining knowledge (skill, ability).

Further, it is suggested that there are two types of invariants that are specified through experience. Those features that are more or less invariant across different activities constitute our knowledge about those objects or events; the invariants across different objects or events constitute the basis of skills and abilities (Figure 7-1).

Figure 7-1. The Relationship between Knowledge and Skills.

Knowledge	Skill
Events Objects	Locomotion Linguistic Representation

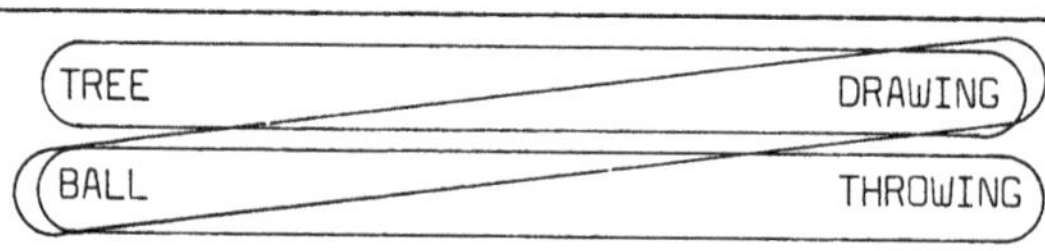

Within this context, Bruner claims that the goal or end-point is crucial in influencing the type of information to be sought and also the skills to be used in obtaining that information. He gives as an example the goal of 'learning about a country' and relates this to learning through direct experience:

> The most obvious way to learn about a country (the goal, or end-point) is to walk its streets, read its poets, eat its foods, work in its fields and so on. In so doing, one will learn both about the country (that the country is poor or hilly, etc.) and how to proceed in the activities required to be of that country (how to mend a net or tell a story). This is surely what is

> meant by learning through one's own direct contingent experience. (Olson and Bruner, 1974, p.130)

Vicarious Experience: Observational Learning

But there are other ways to acquire information eg. from seeing a person struggling with a load one can estimate its weight. In other words, one can experience vicariously and this facility opens up the pathways for learning from a variety of media: films and television, print and the spoken word. Such learning can occur when neither of the primary conditions for learning through contingent experience (self-initiated action or knowledge of its results) is fulfilled.

Bandura (1971) has summarized a wide range of data showing that behaviour can be changed by exposing the learner to modeling stimuli. In his classic 'Bobo doll' experiment (Bandura, 1965) children saw an inflatable plastic clown being abused in a television programme and were then allowed to play with a similar doll. The children were observed to copy the violent acts. Similar work has shown that altruistic behaviour can also be induced by observation of modelled behaviour.

Although early animal studies indicated that learning by observation was confined to higher mammals (Thorndike, 1898) later work has shown this not to be the case. Herbert and Harsh (1944), for example, had two groups of cats learn to pull strings and open doors by observing other cats. One group saw the final error-free performance, the other group saw early error-filled performance. Both groups of cats learned more quickly than the control group, which had not observed another cat's performance.

Bruner (1972) notes that while all animals learn from contingent experience, primates are distinctive in their capacity for learning by observation - there being an enormous amount of observation of adult behaviour by the young. He places great emphasis on the potential of observational learning and particularly the relaxed atmosphere of the social units of the great apes which allow the young to spend extensive periods of time observing techniques, particularly tool-using behaviour, and practising and experimenting with the component acts.

Zimmerman (1977) claims that Bandura's 'Social Learning Theory' (SLT) represents the most sophisticated formulation for human vicarious learning, in that it represents the 'wedding between behavioural and informational processing explanations for human functioning' (p.42). According to SLT observational learning is primarily a cognitive, representational process in which the representations are mentally transformed, stored either symbolically or iconically, and retrieved before being manifested as imitation. Zimmerman argues that it is possible for teachers to use observational learning principles, as described by Bandura, to organize classroom demonstrations to teach concepts and abstract skills to children.

Bruner agrees and indicates that when observational learning is used as an instructional technique in the form of demonstrations the child should be shown critical alternatives and how to choose between them (Olson and Bruner, 1974). Good instruction through modeling depends upon the sensitivity of the instructor to the alternatives likely to be entertained by the child. And, just as providing clear demonstrations involves skill, so it seems probable that learning from demonstrations demands a skill. Modeling may well depend on the capacity not so much to imitate directly as to construct behaviour from already mastered constituent acts in order to match selected features of the model. As an instructional technique modeling in the form of a demonstration is different from a skilled performance.

Vicarious Experience: Symbolic Learning

Bruner acknowledges that a further alternative to learning from direct experience is through symbolically coded information: words, diagrams, maps etc. It is learning through these symbolic systems that most readily substitutes for direct experience in formal schooling. Bruner and Vygotsky have both emphasised the extent to which language provides the means, par excellence, for teaching and learning out of context. Language provides an opportunity for acquiring knowledge in a form compatible with the rules of abstract thought. The human species is marked by its reliance on symbolically coded experience, so much so that language is taken as the distinctive human characteristic, and the development of literacy in various symbolic codes is the primary concern of formalized schooling. The major limitation of all cultural media such as language, numbers, graphs, diagrams etc, is that the information is conveyed through a symbolic system that places a high demand upon literacy in that medium. And the meaning extracted from those symbolic systems will be limited to the meaning acquired by the use of the symbol in the referential or experiential world. In other words, the major limitation of language is that no new information can be conveyed through language - if information falls outside the listener's competence the sentence will be interpreted in terms of knowledge already possessed. Thus, instruction through language is limited to rearranging, ordering and differentiating knowledge or information that the listener has available from other sources (modeling, direct experience). Bruner makes the analogy here with the impossibility of verbally explaining perspective to the blind!

These different forms of experiencing a concept are seen by Bruner as being mapped on to a common underlying structure, or a coherent and generalized concept of reality and the very fact that the representations of reality are partially translatable, one to another, makes instruction possible. Thus, information relevant to action can be acquired by means other than direct action, so that we may learn to sail through watching films and reading books. But the three different forms of experience (enactive, iconic and symbolic) differ greatly in terms of the skills they assume and develop in the learner.

Forms of Instruction

Finally, Bruner suggests that there are three basic forms of instruction all of which provide information relevant to the acquisition of both knowledge and skills and these, in turn, are related to a variety of technological realizations:

1) Systems of arranged contingent experience which are related to structured environments for learning, such as laboratories and experiments, simulations and even educational toys.

2) Systems of observational learning which are associated with demonstrations and modeling, which may be live demonstrations or recordings on film or videotape.

3) Symbolic systems which include such technological realizations as print, drawings, diagrams, graphs and maps.

Thus, Bruner has related our interactions with the world, in terms of the forms of mediation, to the forms of representation which allow our construction of models of the world. These in turn have been related to technological realizations and the development of skills associated with the decoding of communications.

Olson (1976) has taken this further with his theory of instructional means. He makes a distinction between 'utterance' and 'text', in which oral language is characterized as 'a flexible, unspecialized, all-purpose instrument with a low degree of conventionalization' in which meanings are dependent on social relations, context and prior world knowledge of the participants. Written language, with its demands for explicitness of meaning, its permanence and its logical function, serves the cultivation of analytic, scientific and philosophical knowledge. Olsen claims that there is a literacy bias in schools because 'school intelligence' is skill in the medium of text. Clark and Salomon (1986) indicate that such considerations lead to hypotheses concerning further cognitive effects of which may lead to new 'literacy biases' succeeding older ones, for example, as may be the case with computer programming which is a highly structured and analytic activity in a rigidly constrained symbol system.

Cognition, Learning and Media

Salomon (1979) has extended these ideas in his exploration of how symbolic forms cultivate mental skills and affect knowledge acquisition. This acquisition is seen as being mediated by skills of information reception and processing, and because these skills are affected by the nature of the symbol system associated with a given medium, he suggests that each medium may have its own specific effects on how knowledge is extracted.

Salomon takes Olson and Bruner's (1974) 'sought after end' and expands the idea as the 'task to be performed.' He argues that the perception of the task to be performed determines the kind of information one wishes to extract from a coded message. Learning can thus be facilitated to the extent that the activated skills are relevant to the demands of the learning task. He gives as an example a task calling for analytic comparison which activates imagery instead, leading to debilitated learning. Clearly, for effective communication there must be a match between the cognitive demands of the task, the skills required by the codes of the message and the learner's mastery of the codes. There is some evidence which indicates that when certain skills are deficient switching instruction to a medium which places reliance on more highly developed skills or which compensates for the deficiency will enable information to be more readily assimilated.

To demonstrate this Salomon prepared several different versions of a film, which he reasoned would make different demands on the skills available to his fifth-grade subjects. Two versions were produced that were identical except for the fact that the shifts from long-shots to close-ups were accomplished by zoom-ins and outs in the Z version but were left out in the CU version. The Z version was designed to supplant the mental skills of connecting parts and wholes, which the CU version was expected to call upon. Prior to viewing the films the subjects were given a battery of mental tests, including a Detail and Whole Test in which a detail of a drawing was presented alongside the whole object to measure the ability to relate details to perceptual wholes, especially important in the CU version. The results indicated that:

> This difference between the Close-Up/Long-Shot (CU) and ZOOM (Z) correlational patterns strongly suports the expectation that element-specific skill-mastery is required for the acquisition of specific knowledge to the extent that the coding element deviates from the viewer's anticipatory schemata. Indeed, the Close-Up/Long-Shot version seems to call on specific skills, whereas the Zoom version overtly supplants them. Hence, intitial mastery of the relevant skills is far less necessary for knowledge acquistion from the Zoom version. (Salomon, 1979, p.102)

This relates directly to Olson and Bruner's (1974) assertion that knowledge is always mediated through some form of human activity, and the knowledge acquired through such activity has two facets: knowledge about the world and knowledge about the skills involved in gaining the knowledge.

Salomon also found that, at the time that television was being introduced to Israel, heavy viewers of the only children's tv programme (Sesame Street) did better on the Changing Points of View Test. He reasoned from this that a technique which is all pervasive in film and television is the showing of the same scene from different camera angles and repeated exposure to these changes in physical points of view develops skill in shifting points of view in the mind.

A similar effect was observed with Salomon's Space Construction Test. The task is to put four pieces of a picture together so that they form a room. Children who did well on this test were also found to be better able to understand edited films. Salomon reasoned that this is because of visual techniques that are intrinsic to film and television. Three-dimensional space is divided up by pans or cuts in films rather than revealing the whole in one shot. To have a sense of the whole the viewer must mentally integrate the various elements, and commerce with this form of coding information develops the necessary cognitve skill, which enables information to be extracted from the communication.

Implicit in this reasoning is the idea that the symbol system associated with a given medium may produce cognitive changes which result in the cultivation of certain mental skills. Salomon suggests that this is the case with language, which appears to prime cognitive operations, even to trigger them. This receives support from Vygotsky (1962), and Luria (1978) and is in line with Bruner, Olver and

Greenfield's (1966) claim that amplifiers of human capacities must produce an appropriate internal counterpart to be effective. Language is not, however, the only symbol system which participates in cognition and Salomon indicates that it should be possible to learn to think in graphic codes and he quotes the work of Hatano, Miyake and Binks (1977) which shows that expert abacus users internalize the operations of the abacus. Intermediate users still use visible finger movements to accompany mental calculations and if prevented from doing so their performance is impeded. Here the finger movements would appear to have a similar function to Vygotsky's egocentric speech, which is also on route to becoming totally internalized.

If symbol systems of media are to cultivate mental skills, as Salomon suggests, what are the psychological mechanisms involved? He indicates three ways in which cognition can be affected: (1) activation of skills that transform external codes into internal ones (2) short-circuiting skills by overtly providing the end result of mental tranformations that the learner should have employed and (3) overt supplantation, or modeling, of transformational procedures. Each of these have been shown to have a different effect on skill facilitation (Salomon, 1979). Coding elements that activate skills facilitate skill-mastery in already skillful learners; coding elements that short-circuit skills will have little cultivating effects; and coding elements that overtly model skills facilitate skill-mastery in intially unskillful learners.

Although Salomon's work has investigated symbolic codes in film and television, other media have also been shown to develop skills which are transferable. Gagnon (1985) found that giving Harvard College students 5 hours of arcade-game play improved their performance on a standardized paper-and-pencil test of visual-spatial ability, the games serving something like a remedial function for people with relatively undeveloped spatial skills. Greenfield (1987) has also demonstrated a carry-over from video game practice to tests which involved scientific-technical thinking, although novices, with only 2.5 hours practice, performed on the transfer task as well as expert games players with hundreds of hours practice. It has also been suggested that in learning to programme computers pupils will acquire powerfully general higher cognitive skills such as planning abilities, problem-solving heuristics, and 'reflectiveness on the revisionary character of the problem solving process itself.' However, Pea and Kurland (1984) caution against too much optimism and indicate that this is an old idea in a new form: similar arguments have been offered in centuries past for the beneficial cognitive consequences of other powerful symbolic systems, including mathematics, logic, writing systems and even Latin!

A New Direction for Educational Technology

Fosnot (1984) suggested that for most of its history, educational technology has attempted to justify and verify its own basic assumption that both the processes of technology and the products of technology can help improve instructional effectiveness. This has led to a systems approach to instructional design which is grounded in empiricism. However, educational technology need not remain in this position and Fosnot calls for educational technologists to come to terms with the new ideas in cognitive psychology, particularly those of constructivist psychology. Winn (1982) expresses a similar concern with instructional technology and concludes that research in cognitive psychology is further ahead than the application of research findings in instructional design. For many years the work of Piaget and Bruner, the very foundations of much exciting thinking in cognitive psychology, has been largely ignored in the field of educational technology. Now, thanks to the pioneering drive of such researchers as Papert and Salomon the new educational technology is inextricably linked to the 'booming, buzzing' world of cognitive psychology.

REFERENCES

Anschutz, R. (1961) 'August Kekule'. In E. Farber (Ed) Great Chemists. New York: Interscience Publishers.

Bandura, A. (1965) 'Influences of models' reinforcement contingencies on the acquisition of imitative response', Journal of Personality and Social Psychology, 1, 589-595.

Bandura, A. (1971) Social Learning Theory. New York: General Learning Press.

Bruner, J.S. (1960) The Process of Education. Cambridge Mass.: Harvard University Press.

Bruner, J.S. (1964) 'The course of cognitive growth', American Psychologist, 19, 1-15.

Bruner, J.S. (1966a) 'Some Elements of Discovery'. In L.S. Shulman & E.R. Keislar (Eds) Learning by Discovery. Chicago: Rand McNally.

Bruner, J.S. (1966b) Toward a Theory of Instruction. Cambridge, Mass.: Harvard University Press.

Bruner, J.S. (1972) 'Nature and uses of immaturity', American Psychologist, Aug., 687-708.

Bruner, J.S. (1983) In Search of Mind. London: Harper and Row.

Bruner, J.S., Olver, R.R. and Greenfield, P.M. (1966) Studies in Cognitive Growth. Wiley: New York.

Clark, R.E. and Salomon, G. (1986) 'Media in teaching'. In M.C. Wittrock (Ed) Handbook of Research on Teaching (3rd Edition). New York: MacMillan.

Dale, E. (1969) Audiovisual Methods in Teaching (3rd Edition). London: Holt, Rinehart and Winston.

Donaldson, M. (1978) Children's Minds. Glasgow: Fontana /Collins.

Fosnot, C.T. (1984) 'Media and technology in education: a constructivist view', Educational Communication and Technology Journal, 32, 195-205.

Gagnon, D. (1985) 'Videogames and spatial skills: an exploratory study', Educational Communication and Technology Journal, 33(4), 263-275.

Greenfield, P.M. (1987) 'Electronic Technologies, Education and Cognitive Development'. In D.E. Berger, K. Pezdek and W.P. Banks (Eds) Applications of Cognitive Psychology: Problem Solving, Education and Computing. London: Erlbaum.

Greenfield, P.M. and Bruner, J.S. (1966) 'Culture and cognitive growth', International Journal of Psychology, 1(2), 89-107.

Hadamard, J. (1945) An Essay on the Psychology of Invention in the Mathematical Field. New Jersey: Princeton University Press.

Hatano, G., Miyake, Y. and Binks, M.G. (1977) 'Performance of expert abacus operators', Cognition, 5, 57-71.

Herbert, J.J. and Harsh, C.M. (1944) 'Observational learning by cat', Journal of Comparative Psychology, 37, 81-95.

Luria, A.R. (1976) Cognitive Development: Its Cultural and Social Foundations. Cambridge, Massachusetts: Harvard University Press.

Luria, A.R. (1978) The Selected Writings of A.R. Luria. Edited by M. Cole. New York: M.E. Sharpe.

Olson, D.R. (1976) 'Towards a theory of instructional means', Educational Psychologist, 12, 14-35.

Olson, D.R. (1977) 'From utterance to text: the bias of language in speech and writing', Harvard Educational Review, 47(3), 257-281.

Olson, D.R. and Bruner, J.S. (1974) 'Learning Through Experience and Learning Through Media'. In D. R. Olson (Ed) Media and Symbols: The Form Of Expression, Communication, and Education. The Seventy-third Yearbook of the National Society for the Study of Education. Chicago: University of Chicago Press.

Pea, R.D., and Kurland, D.M. (1984) 'On the cognitive effects of learning computer programming', New Ideas in Psychology, 2(2), 137-168.

Piaget, J. (1971) Biology and Knowledge. Chicago: Chicago University Press.

Salomon, G. (1979) Interaction of Media, Cognition and Learning. London: Jossey-Bass.

Scribner, S. and Cole, M. (1981) The Psychology of Literacy. Cambridge, Massachusetts: Harvard University Press.
Thorndike, E.L. (1898) 'Animal Intelligence', Psychological Review, Monograph Supplement, 2, No. 8.
Vygotsky, L.S. (1962) Thought and Language. London: John Wiley.
Wartofsky, M.W. (1983) 'From Genetic Epistemology to Historical Epistemology: Kant, Marx and Piaget'. In L.S. Liben (Ed) Piaget and the Foundations of Knowledge. London: Lawrence Erlbaum.
Washburn, S.L. and Howell, F.C (1960) 'Human Evolution and Culture'. In S. Tax (Ed) The Evolution of Man, Volume 2. Chicago: University of Chicago Press.
Watson, J.D. (1968) The Double Helix; A Personal Account of the Discovery of the Structure of DNA. London: Weidenfeld and Nicolson.
Winn, W. (1982) 'Visualization in learning and instruction: A cognitive effect', Educational Communication and Technology Journal, 30(1), 3-25 .
Zimmerman, B. J. (1977) 'Modeling'. In H. L. Hom and P. A. Robinson (Eds) Psychological Processes in Early Education. London: Academic Press.

INDEX